DATE DUE

Demco No. 62-0549

THE OLD TESTAMENT

Books by Marguerite de Angeli

BLACK FOX OF LORNE

BOOK OF NURSERY AND MOTHER GOOSE RHYMES

BRIGHT APRIL

COPPER-TOED BOOTS

THE DOOR IN THE WALL

ELIN'S AMERIKA

HENNER'S LYDIA

JUST LIKE DAVID

THE OLD TESTAMENT

PETITE SUZANNE

SKIPPACK SCHOOL

A SUMMER DAY WITH TED AND NINA

TED AND NINA HAVE A HAPPY RAINY DAY

TED AND NINA GO TO THE GROCERY STORE

THEE, HANNAH!

UP THE HILL

YONIE WONDERNOSE

The Old Testament

Arranged and illustrated by

MARGUERITE DE ANGELI

With a preface by Samuel Terrien

AUBURN PROFESSOR OF OLD TESTAMENT, UNION THEOLOGICAL SEMINARY

DOUBLEDAY & COMPANY, INC., GARDEN CITY, NEW YORK

THIS BOOK IS DEDICATED

TO ALL OF MY GRANDCHILDREN,

TO MY HUSBAND, DAI DE ANGELI,

AND TO NINA'S HUSBAND, ALFRED KUHN,

WHO KEPT THE HOMES WHILE WE WERE GONE

Library of Congress Catalog Card Number 60-11621
Copyright © 1959, 1960 by Marguerite de Angeli
All Rights Reserved
Printed in the United States of America
Designed by Alma Reese Cardi

CONTENTS

ILLUSTRATOR'S NOTE

As I think back to my early love for the Old Testament stories, I remember a large book, too heavy to hold but convenient to look at while lying on the floor. The pictures in the book are inextricably mixed with those of another large book, Dante's *Inferno,* some of which gave me a delicious thrill of terror. Whatever the book was, and it may have been Doré's *Story of the Bible,* it was a source of unfailing interest. The figures of the patriarchs stood forth majestically, their nobility and towering concept of God overshadowing human fault or foible. Abraham has always been to me a magnificent figure of a man, standing under the starry sky trying to comprehend the infinite. I loved the stories of Ruth and of Esther; of Noah and the flood; of Jacob's dream and his love of Rachel; of Isaac and the beautiful Rebekah. It is impossible to say how early the Old Testament became a part of my life, nor how long the pictures of places and people have been in my mind.

At last, Margaret Lesser of Doubleday & Company gave me an opportunity to put these pictures into a book. Then, in preparation for it, my daughter Nina and I went to the Middle East to get the feeling of time and place; to see the palm and olive trees, to feel the burning sun and the coolness of the heights; to appreciate the value of water and what it must have meant to a traveler to have his dusty feet washed as a gesture of hospitality. On our way to Damascus we stopped at Baalbek, where amid the glorious ruins of ancient Roman temples there stands a still more ancient altar to the god Baal, its deep pit open to the sky and dropping down into the darkness of great sluices beneath the marble floor which carried off the refuse from sacrificial beasts. All day, as we journeyed, the Lebanese mountains, which we had crossed, rose high against the blue sky, Mount Hermon far away and forever snow-capped.

In Damascus we threaded the narrow streets by moonlight, visited a palace courtyard scented with jasmine, saw a weaver at his loom weaving intricately patterned brocade. In a special exhibit we saw the sort of Bedouin tent in which Abraham might have lived with Sarah, his wife, the skin bottle hanging from the tent pole, the jars for meal and oil standing in the cooking place, the skins and robes in the sleeping place.

In Egypt we stood close to the pyramids, built thousands of years ago by the enslaved Hebrews. We crossed the Nile and journeyed to the Valley of the Kings; felt the scorching heat at midday and saw ibis flying to their nests at dusk. In our swift flight by plane from Egypt to Jordanian Jerusalem we passed over the Sea of Reeds and the wilderness where the Children of Israel wandered with Moses for forty years; where the Tables of the Law were handed down and where, when food was scarce, the people murmured against God and longed for the fleshpots of Egypt.

It was a moving experience to see with our own eyes the rock, sacred to all religions, where, it is said, Abraham took Isaac for sacrifice, and where the ram had been provided instead.

Going out from Jerusalem, we traveled over the hills eastward toward Jericho. We left the road and climbed to the top of a hill from which we could see, across the ravine, the source of the brook Cherith. It came out of the side of the opposite cliff and poured in a thin stream down the barren hill, making a path of green. It flowed through the ravine past the cavern which had sheltered Elijah and where he had been fed by the ravens. Now the brook is carried by a small aqueduct to provide water for modern Jericho.

Just beyond the village is a mound through which archaelogists are digging and have found, deep below the surface, the walls of ancient Jericho. We stood looking down through layer upon layer of former civilizations, trying to visualize the most ancient. Then we saw women coming to the well nearby with water jars on their veiled heads, dressed as they had been dressed a thousand years ago. There we ate oranges grown in the valley, then drove on in the noonday heat toward the river Jordan and to the Dead Sea, where we bathed in the bitter waters.

After a time in and around the old city of Jerusalem, most of which is in Jordan, we passed through into Israeli Jerusalem to see the tomb of David and some of the new city, then went on to Tel Aviv. From there we journeyed north, passing many place names long familiar: Bashan, Caesarea, Mount Carmel, and on through the Plain of Jezreel. Just there, on the rise of the hill, Ahab's palace once stood. Not far off is the village of Endor, where lived the witch consulted by King Saul. Rising high above the plain is Mount Tabor and we think of Deborah, Barak, Sisera, and Jael. Every mile of the way to North Galilee is crowded with history and remembrance.

Our sojourn in the biblical lands left us with a sense of the continuity of life and of the reality of the events and characters of the Bible. We walked where they had walked, felt the dust of the road and the heat of the day.

After our return, the images which had always been in my mind remained, but now there was added a background of barren hills and fertile valleys, of rocky plains and an all-pervading light.

If my concept differs from others, it must be so. To me, Adam and Eve are eternally young; Jacob sleeping as I pictured him, with the ladder of light on which angels ascend and descend. In my mind the Angel of Death carries in his hand a brush of twigs, and so I made it, though I can't tell why.

Completing this book has been a long and exacting task but I had the encouragement and patient companionship of my husband as I worked and the advice of Dr. Samuel Terrien and the help of Ann Durell, without whom it could not have had two features which distinguish it from other Old Testaments: its condensation and arrangement according to history.

Marguerite de Angeli

PREFACE

Any literature needs to be read in the light of the history that gave it birth. The Old Testament is no exception. It is a library of thirty-nine books, written in the course of a thousand years or more, and it reflects the life and faith of the Hebrew people from its origins to the time of the Maccabees (about 1275–150 B.C.). Over such an extended period of time, historical conditions changed considerably, and the books of the Old Testament have to be understood in the light of these changes.

For example, nomads sheltered in tents and living chiefly on milk or cheese do not look at life in the same way as farmers who cultivate fields, orchards, and vineyards. Peasants, in turn, are different from city dwellers who are engaged in industry and commerce. Hebrew religion was transformed in the course of the centuries, and the stories of the Patriarchs differ markedly from the reflections of Ecclesiastes or the visions of Daniel.

Nevertheless, beyond the diversity of beliefs and cultic acts, the books of the Old Testament show a remarkable unity of faith. The Hebrews trusted in a God who, unlike the gods of the nations that surrounded them, was the sole creator of the universe and the master of history. They did not use that God as a tool which they possessed. Rather, they felt themselves to be God's special possession, an instrument of God's purpose for the peace of mankind. The unity of the Old Testament may be seen in the promise made to Abraham: "in thee shall all families of the earth be blessed" (Gen. 12:3).

This abbreviated edition of the Old Testament does not follow rigorously the traditional order of the King James Version, but it generally preserves the sequence of the Hebrew Bible, which is in many ways closer to the chronological growth of the literature.

PART I: IN THE BEGINNING: The first story of creation (Gen. 1:1–2:4a) is actually more modern than the second (Gen. 2:4b–3:24). The latter is ancient and was published in David's time as an austere warning against the shallow optimism of a prosperous nation. "Dust thou art, and unto dust shalt thou return" (Gen. 3:19). The former, on the contrary, was told during the Babylonian exile, four centuries later, when people were in despair, to remind them that the world was good and that man had been created in God's image (Gen. 1:25–28). The stories of Cain and Abel, Noah and the Ark, and the Tower of Babel describe the plight of the human race, locked in competition and endless warfare, as a background to the call of Abraham, the father of a new society of men in history.

PART II: THE PATRIARCHS: The ancestors of Israel were described in realistic terms. They were men of faith, but their weaknesses and failures were not concealed. Abraham, Isaac, Jacob, and Joseph moved from Mesopotamia to Egypt, where their descendants became enslaved.

PART III: THE BIRTH OF ISRAEL: With Moses and the Exodus, the Hebrews formed Israel, the "holy people" (about 1275 B.C.). The covenant ("testament") was a marriage that bound them together with their God as a nation set apart from all others for the fulfillment of a special purpose in history. They wandered in the wilderness and at last conquered the land of Canaan (thirteenth to eleventh centuries B.C.).

PART IV: DAVID AND SOLOMON: With David of Bethlehem and his son Solomon, the tribes were organized into a united kingdom and the nation obtained material security. In Jerusalem, Solomon built a temple, where God "sojourned in thick darkness," close to his people and yet outside their reach. After the death of Solomon (922 B.C.), northerners and southerners drifted apart and formed the two kingdoms of Israel (north) and Judah (south).

PART V: THE PROPHETS: During the centuries of the divided monarchy, prophets arose, calling in vain upon Israel and Judah to reform their national life from religious and social corruption. The Israelites were wiped out by the Assyrians (722 B.C.). A century and a half later Jerusalem was destroyed, the temple was burned, and the Judeans were exiled to Mesopotamia by the Babylonians (586 B.C.).

PART VI: THE BABYLONIAN EXILE: Unlike the Israelites of the northern kingdom, who were assimilated into foreign culture and disappeared from history, the Judeans remained together and became the Jews. This extraordinary survival was chiefly due to the influence of Jeremiah, who announced "a new covenant," and of Ezekiel, who saw the rebirth of the nation as a religious community. The poet of Job asked the question, "Is it for nothing that we serve God?" and thus showed the meaning of pure faith. The anonymous prophet, whose poems are preserved in Isaiah 40–55, redefined the mission of the holy people by calling Israel "a light unto the nations" and "the suffering servant of the Lord."

When the Persians conquered Babylon, Cyrus allowed the Jews to return to their land (538 B.C.).

PART VII: THE RESTORATION: While many Jews settled down throughout the Persian Empire and formed the synagogue, a few priestly families returned to Zion and built there a second temple (519–517 B.C.). The Jewish province, under Persian rule, met with hard times. At last Nehemiah restored the walls of Jerusalem (444 B.C.).

During the centuries of the restoration most of the Old Testament books received their final form. The Pentateuch (Genesis to Deuteronomy) was edited as a continuous work and read as "the Law" by Ezra the scribe (397 B.C.). Some Jews, wishing to preserve the purity of the race in the midst of hostile neighbors, compelled their fellows to divorce foreign wives. Sporadic persecution against Jewish communities scattered throughout the Persian Empire produced at times, as in the Book of Esther, a reaction of withdrawal from hostile foreigners. The books of Ruth and Jonah were written as protests against racial isolation and legal strictness; they called for brotherhood among all men. At the same time the poems of the Prophets were collected, and the Psalms, some of which went back to David, were published as the hymnal of the second temple.

PART VIII: THE GREEK RULE AND THE MACCABEES: After the conquest of the Persian Empire by Alexander of Macedonia (333 B.C.) the Jews passed under Greek rule. Under the persecution of Antiochus Ephiphanes they won, through the Maccabees, their political independence (160 B.C.), but they lost it once more under the Romans (63 B.C.). The Old Testament ended with the Book of Daniel, written during the Maccabean struggle, when the ancient hope for a kingdom of justice and peace was still alive. In a deep sense the Bible is the history of God, "always calling aloud, by cry, deed, death and destitution," and saying tirelessly, "Man, where art thou?"

Samuel Terrien

THE OLD TESTAMENT

IN THE BEGINNING

In the beginning God created the heaven and the earth. And the earth was without form, and void; and darkness was upon the face of the deep. And the spirit of God moved upon the face of the waters.

And God said, "Let there be light." And there was light. And God saw the light, that it was good; and God divided the light from the darkness. And God called the light Day and the darkness he called Night.

And God said, "Let the earth bring forth the living creature after his kind, cattle and creeping thing and beast of the earth after his kind." And it was so.

And God said, "Let us make man in our image, after our likeness; and let them have dominion over the fish of the sea and over the fowl of the air and over the cattle and over all the earth and over every creeping thing that creepeth upon the earth." So God created man in his own image, in the image of God created he him; male and female created he them.

And the Lord God planted a garden eastward in Eden; and there he put the man whom he had formed. And out of the ground made the Lord God to grow every tree that is pleasant to the sight and good for food; the tree of life also in the midst of the garden, and the tree of knowledge of good and evil. And a river went out of Eden to water the garden. And the Lord God took the man and put him into the garden of Eden to dress it and to keep it.

And the Lord God commanded the man, saying, "Of every tree of the garden thou mayest freely eat, but of the tree of the knowledge of good and evil, thou shalt not eat of it, for in the day that thou eatest thereof thou shalt surely die."

Now the serpent was more subtil than any beast of the field which the Lord God had made. And he said unto the woman, "Yea, hath God said ye shall not eat of every tree of the garden?"

And the woman said unto the serpent, "We may eat of the fruit of the trees of the garden, but of the fruit of the tree which is in the midst of the garden, God hath said: 'Ye shall not eat of it, neither shall ye touch it, lest ye die.'"

And the serpent said unto the woman, "Ye shall not surely die, for God doth know that in the day ye eat thereof, then your eyes shall be opened and ye shall be as gods, knowing good and evil."

And when the woman saw that the tree was good for food and that it was pleasant to the eyes, and a tree to be desired to make one wise, she took of the fruit thereof and did eat, and gave also unto her husband with her and he did

THE GARDEN OF EDEN

eat. And the eyes of them both were opened, and they knew that they were naked; and they sewed fig leaves together and made themselves aprons. And they heard the voice of the Lord God walking in the garden in the cool of the day, and Adam and his wife hid themselves from the presence of the Lord God amongst the trees of the garden.

And the Lord God called unto Adam and said unto him, "Where art thou?"

And he said, "I heard thy voice in the garden and I was afraid, because I was naked; and I hid myself."

And he said, "Who told thee that thou wast naked? Hast thou eaten of the tree whereof I commanded thee that thou shouldest not eat?"

Adam and Eve

And the man said, "The woman whom thou gavest to be with me, she gave me of the tree, and I did eat."

And the Lord God said unto the woman, "What is this that thou hast done?"

And the woman said, "The serpent beguiled me and I did eat."

And the Lord God said unto the serpent, "Because thou hast done this thou art cursed above all cattle and above every beast of the field."

And unto Adam he said, "Because thou hast hearkened unto the voice of thy wife and hast eaten of the tree, of which I commanded thee, saying, 'Thou shalt not eat of it,' cursed is the ground for thy sake. In sorrow shalt thou eat of it all the days of thy life; thorns also and thistles shall it bring forth to thee; and thou shalt eat the herb of the field; in the sweat of thy face shalt thou eat bread."

Adam and Eve GENESIS

And Adam called his wife's name Eve because she was the mother of all living. Unto Adam also and to his wife did the Lord God make coats of skins, and clothed them.

And the Lord God said, "Behold, the man is become as one of us, to know good and evil. And now, lest he put forth his hand, and take also of the tree of life, and eat, and live for ever." Therefore the Lord God sent him forth from the garden of Eden to till the ground. So he drove out the man and he placed at the east of the garden of Eden cherubims, and a flaming sword which turned every way, to keep the way of the tree of life.

CAIN AND ABEL BRING OFFERINGS UNTO THE LORD

And Eve bare Cain, and said, "I have gotten a man from the Lord."

And she again bare his brother Abel. And Abel was a keeper of sheep, but Cain was a tiller of the ground. And in process of time it came to pass that Cain brought of the fruit of the ground an offering unto the Lord. And Abel, he also brought of the firstlings of his flock and of the fat thereof. And the Lord had respect unto Abel and to his offering, but unto Cain and to his offering he had not respect. And Cain was very wroth and his countenance fell.

And the Lord said unto Cain, "Why art thou wroth and why is thy countenance fallen? If thou doest well, shalt thou not be accepted? And if thou doest not well, sin lieth at the door. And unto thee shall be his desire and thou shalt rule over him."

And Cain talked with Abel his brother. And it came to pass, when they were in the field, that Cain rose up against Abel his brother and slew him.

And the Lord said unto Cain, "Where is Abel thy brother?"

And he said, "I know not. Am I my brother's keeper?"

And he said, "What hast thou done? The voice of thy brother's blood crieth unto me from the ground. And now art thou cursed from the earth, which hath opened her mouth to receive thy brother's blood from thy hand: when thou tillest the ground, it shall not henceforth yield unto thee her strength; a fugitive and a vagabond shalt thou be in the earth."

And Cain said unto the Lord, "My punishment is greater than I can bear."

There were giants in the earth in those days. And God saw that the wickedness of man was great in the earth, and that every imagination of the thoughts of his heart was only evil continually.

And the Lord said, "I will destroy man whom I have created from the face of the earth."

Noah was a just man and perfect in his generations, and Noah walked with God. And Noah begat three sons, Shem, Ham, and Japheth.

And God said unto Noah, "Make thee an ark of gopher wood; rooms shalt thou make in the ark, and shalt pitch it within and without with pitch. And this is the fashion which thou shalt make it of. The length of the ark shall be three hundred cubits, the breadth of it fifty cubits, and the height of it thirty cubits. A window shalt thou make to the ark, and in a cubit shalt thou finish it above; and the door of the ark shalt thou set in the side thereof. With lower, second, and third stories shalt thou make it.

"And behold, I, even I, do bring a flood of waters upon the earth, to destroy all flesh, wherein is the breath of life, from under heaven; and every thing that is in the earth shall die. But with thee will I establish my covenant, and thou shalt come into the ark, thou and thy sons and thy wife and thy sons' wives with thee. And of every living thing of all flesh, two of every sort shalt thou bring into the ark, to keep them alive with thee; they shall be male and female. Of fowls after their kind, and of cattle after their kind, of every creeping thing of the earth after his kind, two of every sort shall come unto thee, to keep them alive. And take thou

THE ANIMALS ENTER NOAH'S ARK

unto thee of all food that is eaten, and thou shalt gather it to thee; and it shall be for food for thee and for them."

Thus did Noah; according to all that God commanded him, so did he. And it came to pass after seven days that the waters of the flood were upon the earth. In the selfsame day entered Noah, and Shem and Ham and Japheth, the sons of Noah, and Noah's wife and the three wives of his sons with them, into the ark; they, and every beast after his kind, and all the cattle after their kind.

And the flood was forty days upon the earth; and the waters increased and bare up the ark, and it was lifted up above the earth. And the waters prevailed upon the earth an hundred and fifty days.

And God remembered Noah, and every living thing, and all the cattle that was with him in the ark; and God made a wind to pass over the earth and the waters assuaged. And the ark rested in the seventh month, on the seventeenth day of the month, upon the mountains of Ararat.

And it came to pass at the end of forty days that Noah opened the window of the ark which he had made, and he sent forth a raven, which went forth to and fro, until the

waters were dried up from off the earth. Also he sent forth
a dove from him, to see if the waters were abated from off
the face of the ground; but the dove found no rest for the sole
of her foot, and she returned unto him into the ark, for the
waters were on the face of the whole earth. Then he put
forth his hand and took her and pulled her in unto him into
the ark.

And he stayed yet other seven days, and again he sent
forth the dove out of the ark. And the dove came in to him
in the evening, and, lo, in her mouth was an olive leaf
plucked off. So Noah knew that the waters were abated from
off the earth. And he stayed yet other seven days and sent
forth the dove, which returned not again unto him any more.

And Noah built an altar unto the Lord. And the
Lord smelled a sweet savour, and the Lord said in his heart,
"I will not again curse the ground any more for man's sake.
While the earth remaineth, seedtime and harvest, and cold
and heat, and summer and winter, and day and night shall
not cease. And I will establish my covenant with you; neither
shall all flesh be cut off any more by the waters of a flood;
neither shall there any more be a flood to destroy the earth."

And God said, "This is the token of the covenant which
I make between me and you and every living creature that
is with you, for perpetual generations: I do set my bow in
the cloud and it shall be for a token of a covenant between
me and the earth."

*Noah and
the Ark*
GENESIS
25

And the whole earth was of one language and of one speech. And it came to pass, as the children of men journeyed from the east, that they found a plain in the land of Shinar; and they dwelt there.

And they said one to another, "Go to, let us make brick and burn them thoroughly." And they had brick for stone, and slime had they for mortar.

And they said, "Go to, let us build us a city and a tower whose top may reach unto heaven; and let us make us a name, lest we be scattered abroad upon the face of the whole earth."

And the Lord came down to see the city and the tower which the children of men builded.

And the Lord said, "Behold, the people is one, and they have all one language, and this they begin to do. And now nothing will be restrained from them which they have imagined to do. Go to, let us go down, and there confound their language, that they may not understand one another's speech."

So the Lord scattered them abroad from thence upon the face of all the earth; and they left off to build the city. Therefore is the name of it called Babel, because the Lord did there confound the language of all the earth, and from thence did the Lord scatter them abroad upon the face of all the earth.

THE PATRIARCHS

Terah took Abram, his son, and Lot, the son of Haran (his son's son), and Sarai, his daughter-in-law, his son Abram's wife; and they went forth with them from Ur of the Chaldees to go into the land of Canaan; and they came unto Haran and dwelt there.

Now the Lord had said unto Abram, "Get thee out of thy country, and from thy kindred, and from thy father's house, unto a land that I will shew thee; and I will make of thee a great nation, and I will bless thee and make thy name great; and thou shalt be a blessing. And I will bless them that bless thee and curse him that curseth thee; and in thee shall all families of the earth be blessed."

So Abram departed, as the Lord had spoken unto him; and Lot went with him. And Abram was seventy and five years old when he departed out of Haran. And Abram took Sarai, his wife, and Lot, his brother's son, and all their substance that they had gathered, and the souls that they had gotten in Haran; and they went forth to go into the land of Canaan; and into the land of Canaan they came.

And Abram journeyed, going on still toward the south. And Abram was very rich in cattle, in silver, and in gold. And he went on his journeys from the south even to Bethel,

Abraham Comes to Canaan
GENESIS
27

unto the place where his tent had been at the beginning, between Bethel and Hai, unto the place of the altar, which he had made there at the first. And there Abram called on the name of the Lord.

And there was a strife between the herdmen of Abram's cattle and the herdmen of Lot's cattle.

And Abram said unto Lot, "Let there be no strife, I pray thee, between me and thee, and between my herdmen and thy herdmen, for we be brethren. Is not the whole land before thee? Separate thyself, I pray thee, from me; if thou wilt take the left hand, then I will go to the right, or if thou depart to the right hand, then I will go to the left."

Then Lot chose him all the plain of Jordan; and Lot journeyed east, and they separated themselves the one from the other. And Abram dwelt in the land of Canaan, and Lot dwelled in the cities of the plain and pitched his tent toward Sodom. Then Abram removed his tent and came and dwelt in the plain of Mamre, which is in Hebron, and built there an altar unto the Lord.

And the Lord brought him forth abroad and said, "Look now toward heaven and tell the stars, if thou be able to number them." And he said unto him, "So shall thy seed be."

ABRAM LEAVES LOT

Now Sarai, Abram's wife, bare him no children; and she had an handmaid, an Egyptian, whose name was Hagar. And Sarai, Abram's wife, took Hagar, her maid, the Egyptian, after Abram had dwelt ten years in the land of Canaan, and gave her to her husband Abram to be

his wife. And her mistress was despised in her eyes. And when Sarai dealt hardly with her, she fled from her face. And the angel of the Lord found her by a fountain of water in the wilderness.

And the angel of the Lord said unto her, "Return to thy mistress and submit thyself under her hands." And the angel of the Lord said unto her, "I will multiply thy seed exceedingly, that it shall not be numbered for multitude." And the angel of the Lord said unto her, "Behold, thou art with child and shalt bear a son, and shalt call his name Ishmael."

And Hagar bare Abram a son; and Abram called his son's name, which Hagar bare, Ishmael.

When Abram was ninety years old and nine, the Lord appeared to Abram and said unto him, "I am the Almighty God; walk before me and be thou perfect."

And Abram fell on his face, and God talked with him, saying: "As for me, behold, my covenant is with thee, and thou shalt be a father of many nations. Neither shall thy name any more be called Abram, but thy name shall be Abraham, for a father of many nations have I made thee. As for Sarai, thy wife, thou shalt not call her name Sarai, but Sarah shall her name be. And I will bless her and give thee a son also of her; yea, I will bless her, and she shall be a mother of nations; kings of people shall be of her."

And the Lord appeared unto Abraham in the plains of Mamre; and he sat in the tent door in the heat of the day. And he lifted up his eyes and looked, and, lo, three men stood by him.

And when he saw them he ran to meet them from the tent door and bowed himself toward the ground and said, "My Lord, if now I have found favour in thy sight, pass not away, I pray thee, from thy servant; let a little water, I pray you, be fetched, and wash your feet and rest yourselves under

Hagar
GENESIS

Isaac is Born
GENESIS
31

the tree. And I will fetch a morsel of bread and comfort ye your hearts; after that ye shall pass on. For therefore are ye come to your servant."

And they said, "So do, as thou hast said."

And Abraham hastened into the tent unto Sarah and said, "Make ready quickly three measures of fine meal, knead it, and make cakes upon the hearth."

And Abraham ran unto the herd and fetched a calf tender and good and gave it unto a young man, and he hasted to dress it. And he took butter and milk and the calf which he had dressed and set it before them; and he stood by them under the tree and they did eat.

And they said unto him, "Where is Sarah, thy wife?"

And he said, "Behold, in the tent."

And the Lord said, "I will certainly return unto thee according to the time of life; and, lo, Sarah, thy wife, shall have a son."

And Sarah heard it in the tent door, which was behind him. Now Abraham and Sarah were old and well stricken in age; therefore Sarah laughed within herself.

And the Lord said unto Abraham, "Wherefore did Sarah laugh, saying, 'Shall I of a surety bear a child, which am old?' Is anything too hard for the Lord?"

And the Lord visited Sarah as he had said, and the Lord did unto Sarah as he had spoken. For Sarah bare Abraham a son in his old age, at the set time of which God had spoken to him. And Abraham called the name of his son, whom Sarah bare to him, Isaac. And Abraham circumcised his son Isaac, being eight days old, as God had commanded him. And Abraham was an hundred years old when his son Isaac was born unto him.

And Sarah said, "God hath made me to laugh, so that all that hear will laugh with me."

SARAH LAUGHS AT THE WORDS OF THE LORD

And the child grew and was weaned, and Abraham made a great feast the same day that Isaac was weaned. And Sarah saw the son of Hagar the Egyptian, which she had borne unto Abraham, mocking.

Wherefore she said unto Abraham, "Cast out this bondwoman and her son, for the son of this bondwoman shall not be heir with my son, even with Isaac."

And the thing was very grievous in Abraham's sight because of his son. And Abraham rose up early in the morning, and took bread and a bottle of water, and gave it unto Hagar, putting it on her shoulder, and the child, and sent her away; and she departed and wandered in the wilderness of Beersheba. And the water was spent in the bottle, and she cast the child under one of the shrubs. And she went and sat her down over against him a good way off, as it were a bowshot. For she said:

"Let me not see the death of the child."

And she sat over against him and lifted up her voice and wept. And God opened her eyes and she saw a well of water; and she went and filled the bottle with water and gave the lad drink. And God was with the lad; and he grew and dwelt in the wilderness and became an archer.

It came to pass that God said unto Abraham, "Take now thy son, thine only son Isaac, whom thou lovest, and get thee into the land of Moriah; and offer him there for a burnt offering upon one of the mountains which I will tell thee of."

And Abraham rose up early in the morning and saddled his ass and took two of his young men with him, and Isaac, his son, and clave the wood for the burnt offering, and rose up and went unto the place of which God had told him.

And Abraham said unto his young men, "Abide ye here with the ass, and I and the lad will go yonder and worship and come again to you."

And Abraham took the wood of the burnt offering and laid it upon Isaac, his son; and he took the fire in his hand, and a knife, and they went both of them together.

And Isaac spake unto Abraham, his father, and said, "My father!"

And he said, "Here am I, my son!"

And Isaac said, "Behold the fire and the wood, but where is the lamb for a burnt offering?"

And Abraham said, "My son, God will provide himself a lamb for a burnt offering." So they went both of them together. And they came to the place which God had told him of; and Abraham built an altar there and laid the wood in order and bound Isaac, his son, and laid him on the altar upon the wood. And Abraham stretched forth his hand and took the knife to slay his son.

And the angel of the Lord called unto him out of heaven and said, "Abraham, Abraham!"

And he said, "Here am I!"

And he said, "Lay not thine hand upon the lad, neither do thou any thing unto him, for now I know that thou fearest God, seeing thou hast not withheld thy son, thine only son, from me."

And Abraham lifted up his eyes and looked, and behold behind him a ram caught in a thicket by his horns; and Abraham went and took the ram and offered him up for a burnt offering in the stead of his son.

And Sarah died. And after this Abraham buried Sarah, his wife, in the cave of the field of Machpelah before Mamre.

And Abraham said unto his eldest servant of his house, that ruled over all that he had: "Thou shalt go unto my country, and to my kindred, and take a wife unto my son Isaac."

And the servant took ten camels of the camels of his master and departed, for all the goods of his master were in his hand. And he arose and went to Mesopotamia, unto the city of Nahor. And he made his camels to kneel down without the city by a well of water at the time of the evening, even the time that women go out to draw water.

And he said, "O Lord God of my master Abraham, I pray thee, send me good speed this day and shew kindness unto my master Abraham. Behold, I stand here by the well of water, and the daughters of the men of the city come out to draw water; and let it come to pass that the damsel to whom I shall say, 'Let down thy pitcher, I pray thee, that I may drink,' and she shall say, 'Drink, and I will give thy camels drink also,' let the same be she that thou hast appointed for thy servant Isaac."

And it came to pass, before he had done speaking, that, behold, Rebekah came out, who was born to Bethuel, son of Milcah, the wife of Nahor, Abraham's brother, with her

REBEKAH MEETS ABRAHAM'S SERVANT AT THE WELL

pitcher upon her shoulder. And the damsel was very fair to look upon; and she went down to the well and filled her pitcher and came up.

And the servant ran to meet her and said, "Let me, I pray thee, drink a little water of thy pitcher."

And she said, "Drink, my lord!" And she hasted and let down her pitcher upon her hand and gave him drink. And the man took a golden earring of half a shekel weight, and two bracelets for her hands of ten shekels weight of gold, and said, "Is there room in thy father's house for us to lodge in?"

And she said unto him, "We have both straw and provender enough, and room to lodge in." And the damsel ran and told them of her mother's house these things.

And Rebekah had a brother, and his name was Laban, and Laban ran out unto the man, unto the well. And it came to pass, when he saw the earring and bracelets upon his sister's hands, and when he heard the words of Rebekah, his sister, saying, "Thus spake the man unto me," that he came unto the man, and, behold, he stood by the camels at the well.

And Laban said, "Come in, thou blessed of the Lord. Wherefore standest thou without? For I have prepared the house, and room for the camels."

And the man came into the house, and Laban ungirded his camels and gave straw and provender for the camels, and water to wash his feet, and the men's feet that were with him.

LABAN GIVES THE SERVANT WATER TO WASH HIS FEET

ISAAC FIRST MEETS REBEKAH

And there was set meat before him to eat; but he said:

"I will not eat until I have told mine errand."

And Laban said, "Speak on."

And he said, "I am Abraham's servant. And the Lord God of my master Abraham hath led me in the right way to take my master's brother's daughter unto his son. And now if ye will deal kindly and truly with my master, tell me, and if not, tell me, that I may turn to the right hand or to the left."

Then Laban and Bethuel answered and said, "The thing proceedeth from the Lord; we cannot speak unto thee bad or good. Behold, Rebekah is before thee, take her and go, and let her be thy master's son's wife, as the Lord hath spoken."

And Isaac went out to meditate in the field at the eventide, and he lifted up his eyes and saw, and, behold, the camels were coming. And Rebekah lifted up her eyes and when she saw Isaac she lighted off the camel.

And Isaac brought her into his mother Sarah's tent and she became his wife and he loved her. And Isaac was comforted after his mother's death.

And Isaac entreated the Lord for his wife, because she was barren. And Rebekah went to inquire of the Lord.

And the Lord said unto her, "Two nations are in thy womb."

And when her days to be delivered were fulfilled, behold, there were twins in her womb. And the first came out red, all over like an hairy garment; and they called his name Esau. And after that came his brother out and his hand took hold on Esau's heel; and his name was called Jacob. And the boys grew.

Esau was a cunning hunter, a man of the field, and Jacob was a plain man, dwelling in tents. And Isaac loved Esau because he did eat of his venison, but Rebekah loved Jacob. And Jacob boiled pottage; and Esau came from the field and he was faint.

And Esau said to Jacob, "Feed me, I pray thee, with that same red pottage, for I am faint."

And Jacob said, "Sell me this day thy birthright."

And Esau said, "Behold, I am at the point to die and what profit shall this birthright do to me?"

And Jacob said, "Swear to me this day." And Esau sware unto him and he sold his birthright unto Jacob.

Then Jacob gave Esau bread and pottage of lentiles; and he did eat and drink and rose up and went his way.

And it came to pass that when Isaac was old and his eyes were dim, so that he could not see, he called Esau, his eldest son, and said unto him, "My son!"

And Esau said unto him, "Behold, here am I!"

And Isaac said, "Behold now, I am old, I know not the day of my death. Now therefore take, I pray thee, thy weapons, thy quiver and thy bow, and go out to the field and take me some venison; and make me savoury meat, such as I love, and bring it to me that I may eat, that my soul may bless thee before I die."

And Rebekah heard when Isaac spake to Esau, his son. And Esau went to the field to hunt for venison and to bring it.

And Rebekah spake unto Jacob, her son, saying, "Behold, I heard thy father speak unto Esau, thy brother, saying, 'Bring me venison and make me savoury meat that I may

Esau and Jacob GENESIS 42

eat and bless thee before the Lord before my death.' Now therefore, my son, obey my voice according to that which I command thee. Go now to the flock and fetch me from thence two good kids of the goats, and I will make them savoury meat for thy father, such as he loveth, and thou shalt bring it to thy father, that he may eat, and that he may bless thee before his death."

And Jacob said to Rebekah, his mother, "Behold, Esau, my brother, is a hairy man, and I am a smooth man. My father, peradventure, will feel me, and I shall seem to him as a deceiver, and I shall bring a curse upon me, and not a blessing."

And his mother said unto him, "Upon me be thy curse, my son; only obey my voice and go fetch me them."

And he went and fetched and brought them to his mother, and his mother made savoury meat, such as his father loved. And Rebekah took goodly raiment of her eldest son, Esau, which were with her in the house, and put them upon Jacob, her younger son; and she put the skins of the kids of the goats upon his hands and upon the smooth of his neck. And she gave the savoury meat and the bread, which she had prepared, into the hand of her son Jacob.

And he came unto his father and said, "My father!"

And Isaac said, "Here am I. Who art thou, my son?"

And Jacob said unto his father, "I am Esau, thy first-born; I have done according as thou badest me; arise, I pray thee, sit and eat of my venison, that thy soul may bless me."

And Isaac said unto his son, "How is it that thou hast found it so quickly, my son?"

And he said, "Because the Lord thy God brought it to me."

And Isaac said unto Jacob, "Come near, I pray thee, that I may feel thee, my son, whether thou be my very son

Esau or not."

And Jacob went near unto Isaac, his father; and he felt
him and said, "The voice is Jacob's voice but the hands are

the hands of Esau." And he discerned him not, because his hands were hairy, as his brother Esau's hands; so he blessed him.

And it came to pass, as soon as Isaac had made an end of blessing Jacob, and Jacob was yet scarce gone out from the presence of Isaac, his father, that Esau, his brother, came in from his hunting. And he also had made savoury meat, and brought it unto his father, and said unto his father:

"Let my father arise and eat of his son's venison, that thy soul may bless me."

And Isaac, his father, said unto him, "Who art thou?"

And he said, "I am thy son, thy firstborn Esau."

And Isaac trembled very exceedingly and said, "Who? Where is he that hath taken venison and brought it me, and I have eaten of all before thou camest and have blessed him? Yea, and he shall be blessed!"

And when Esau heard the words of his father he cried with a great and exceeding bitter cry and said unto his father, "Bless me, even me also, O my father!"

And he said, "Thy brother came with subtilty and hath taken away thy blessing!"

And Esau said, "Is not he rightly named Jacob? For he hath supplanted me these two times: he took away my birthright, and, behold, now he hath taken away my blessing." And he said, "Hast thou not reserved a blessing for me?"

And Isaac answered and said unto Esau, "Behold, I have made him thy lord, and all his brethren have I given to him for servants, and with corn and wine have I sustained him. And what shall I do now unto thee, my son?"

And Esau said unto his father, "Hast thou but one blessing, my father? Bless me, even me also, O my father!" And Esau lifted up his voice and wept.

And Esau hated Jacob because of the blessing wherewith his father blessed him. And Esau said in his heart, "The days of mourning for my father are at hand, then will I slay my brother Jacob."

And these words of Esau, her elder son, were told to Rebekah; and she sent and called Jacob, her younger son, and said unto him, "Behold, thy brother Esau, as touching thee, doth comfort himself, purposing to kill thee. Now therefore, my son, obey my voice and arise, flee thou to Laban, my brother, to Haran."

And Jacob went out from Beersheba and went toward Haran. And he lighted upon a certain place and tarried there all night, because the sun was set; and he took of the stones of that place and put them for his pillows and lay down in that place to sleep. And he dreamed and behold a ladder set up on the earth, and the top of it reached to heaven, and behold the angels of God ascending and descending on it.

And, behold, the Lord stood above it and said, "I am the Lord God of Abraham, thy father, and the God of Isaac. The land whereon thou liest, to thee will I give it, and to thy seed."

And Jacob awaked out of his sleep and he said, "Surely the Lord is in this place and I knew it not."

And Jacob rose up early in the morning and took the stone that he had put for his pillows, and set it up for a pillar and poured oil upon the top of it. And he called the name of that place Bethel.

JACOB'S DREAM

Then Jacob went on his journey and came into the land of the people of the east. And he looked and behold a well in the field, and, lo, there were three flocks of sheep lying by it, for out of that well they watered the flocks; and a great stone was upon the well's mouth. And thither were all the flocks gathered; and they rolled the stone from the well's mouth and watered the sheep and put the stone again upon the well's mouth in his place.

And Jacob said unto them, "My brethren, whence be ye?"

And they said, "Of Haran are we."

And he said unto them, "Know ye Laban, the son of Nahor?"

And they said, "We know him."

And he said unto them, "Is he well?"

And they said, "He is well; and, behold, Rachel, his daughter, cometh with the sheep."

And it came to pass, when Jacob saw Rachel, the daughter of Laban, his mother's brother, Jacob went near and rolled the stone from the well's mouth and watered the flock of Laban. And Jacob kissed Rachel and lifted up his voice and wept. And Jacob told Rachel that he was her father's brother and that he was Rebekah's son; and she ran and told her father.

When Laban heard the tidings of Jacob, his sister's son, he ran to meet him and embraced him and kissed him and brought him to his house. And Jacob abode with him the space of a month.

And Laban said unto Jacob, "Shouldst thou serve me for nought? Tell me, what shall thy wages be?"

Laban had two daughters; the name of the elder was Leah and the name of the younger was Rachel. Leah was tender eyed, but Rachel was beautiful and well favoured.

LEAH AND RACHEL

And Jacob loved Rachel and said:

"I will serve thee seven years for Rachel, thy younger daughter."

And Laban said, "It is better that I give her to thee than that I should give her to another man; abide with me."

And Jacob served seven years for Rachel, and they seemed unto him but a few days, for the love he had to her.

And Laban gathered together all the men of the place and made a feast. And it came to pass in the evening that he took Leah, his daughter, and brought her to Jacob; and Laban gave unto his daughter Leah, Zilpah, his maid, for an handmaid. And it came to pass that in the morning, behold, it was Leah.

And Jacob said to Laban, "What is this thou hast done unto me? Did I not serve with thee for Rachel? Wherefore then hast thou beguiled me?"

And Laban said, "It must not be so done in our country, to give the younger before the firstborn. Fulfill her week, and we will give thee this also for the service which thou shalt serve with me yet seven other years."

And Jacob did so. And Laban gave him Rachel, his daughter, to wife also. And Laban gave to Rachel, his daughter, Bilhah, his handmaid, to be her maid. And Jacob loved also Rachel more than Leah, and served with Laban yet seven other years.

And Leah bare a son and she called his name Reuben. And she conceived again and bare a son and she called his name Simeon. And she conceived again and bare a son and his name was called Levi. And she conceived again and bare a son and she called his name Judah.

And when Rachel saw that she bare Jacob no children, Rachel envied her sister. And she gave him Bilhah, her handmaid, to wife. And Bilhah bare Jacob a son. And Rachel called his name Dan. And Bilhah bare Jacob a second son. And Rachel called his name Naphtali.

Leah took Zilpah, her maid, and gave her Jacob to wife. And Zilpah bare Jacob a son. And Leah called his name Gad. And Zilpah bare Jacob a second son. And Leah called his name Asher.

And Leah bare Jacob the fifth son and she called his name Issachar. And Leah bare Jacob the sixth son and she called his name Zebulun. And afterwards she bare a daughter and called her name Dinah.

And God remembered Rachel and she bare a son and said, "God hath taken away my reproach." And she called his name Joseph and said, "The Lord shall add to me another son."

JACOB AND HIS KINDRED ON THE JOURNEY TO CANAAN

And it came to pass, when Rachel had borne Joseph, that Jacob said unto Laban, "Send me away, that I may go unto mine own place and to my country. Give me my wives and my children, for whom I have served thee, and let me go, for thou knowest my service which I have done thee."

And Laban said unto him, "What shall I give thee?"

And Jacob said, "I will pass through all thy flock today, removing from thence all the speckled and spotted cattle, and all the brown cattle among the sheep, and the spotted and speckled among the goats; and of such shall be my hire."

And he heard the words of Laban's sons, saying, "Jacob hath taken away all that was our father's and of that which was our father's hath he gotten all this glory." And Jacob beheld the countenance of Laban and, behold, it was not toward him as before.

And the Lord said unto Jacob, "Return unto the land of thy fathers and to thy kindred, and I will be with thee."

Then Jacob rose up and set his sons and his wives upon camels; and he carried away all his cattle, and all his goods which he had gotten, the cattle of his getting, which he had gotten in Padanaram, for to go to Isaac, his father, in the land of Canaan. And it was told Laban on the third day that Jacob was fled. And he took his brethren with him and pursued after him seven days' journey, and they overtook him in the mount Gilead.

Jacob Leaves Laban
GENESIS
54

And Jacob was wroth, and chode with Laban, and Jacob answered and said to Laban: "What is my trespass?"

And Laban answered and said unto Jacob, "These daughters are my daughters, and these children are my children, and these cattle are my cattle, and all that thou seest is mine; and what can I do this day unto these my daughters or unto their children which they have borne? Now therefore come thou, let us make a covenant, I and thou, and let it be for a witness between me and thee." And Jacob took a stone and set it up for a pillar.

And Jacob said unto his brethren, "Gather stones." And they took stones and made an heap, and they did eat there upon the heap.

And Laban said, "This heap is a witness between me and thee this day."

Therefore was the name of it called Galeed and Mizpah; for he said, "The Lord watch between me and thee when we are absent one from another."

And early in the morning Laban rose up and kissed his sons and his daughters and blessed them; and Laban departed and returned unto his place.

And Jacob went on his way and he called the name of that place Mahanaim. And Jacob sent messengers before him to Esau, his brother, unto the land of Seir, the country of Edom.

And he commanded them, saying, "Thus shall ye speak unto my lord Esau: 'Thy servant Jacob saith thus, "I have sojourned with Laban and stayed there until now; and I have oxen and asses, flocks and menservants and women-servants; and I have sent to tell my lord, that I may find grace in thy sight."'"

And he rose up that night and took his two wives and his two womenservants and his eleven sons, and passed over

JACOB MEETS ESAU AT THE FORD JABBOK

the ford Jabbok. And he took them and sent them over the brook. And Jacob was left alone; and there wrestled a man with him until the breaking of the day.

And the man said, "Let me go, for the day breaketh."

And Jacob said, "I will not let thee go except thou bless me."

And he said unto him, "What is thy name?"

And he said, "Jacob."

And he said, "Thy name shall be called no more Jacob, but Israel, for as a prince hast thou power with God and with men, and hast prevailed."

And Jacob lifted up his eyes and looked and, behold, Esau came, and with him four hundred men. And Esau ran to meet him and embraced him, and fell on his neck and kissed him; and they wept.

Now the sons of Jacob were twelve:

The sons of Leah: Reuben, Jacob's firstborn, and Simeon, and Levi, and Judah, and Issachar, and Zebulun.

The sons of Rachel: Joseph and Benjamin.

And the sons of Bilhah, Rachel's handmaid: Dan and Naphtali.

And the sons of Zilpah, Leah's handmaid: Gad and Asher.

These are the sons of Jacob, which were born to him in Padanaram.

And Jacob came unto Isaac, his father, unto Mamre, unto the city of Arbah, which is Hebron, where Abraham and Isaac sojourned. And the days of Isaac were an hundred and fourscore years. And Isaac gave up the ghost and died, and was gathered unto his people, being old and full of days; and his sons Esau and Jacob buried him.

And Jacob dwelt in the land wherein his father was a stranger, in the land of Canaan.

oseph, being seventeen years old, was feeding the flock with his brethren. Now Israel loved Joseph more than all his children, because he was the son of his old age, and he made him a coat of many colours. And when his brethren saw that their father loved him more than all his brethren they hated him and could not speak peaceably unto him. And Joseph dreamed a dream and he told it his brethren, and they hated him yet the more.

And he said unto them, "Hear, I pray you, this dream which I have dreamed, for, behold, we were binding sheaves in the field and, lo, my sheaf arose and also stood upright; and, behold, your sheaves stood round about and made obeisance to my sheaf."

And his brethren said to him, "Shalt thou indeed reign over us? Or shalt thou indeed have dominion over us?" And they hated him yet the more for his dreams and for his words.

And he dreamed yet another dream and told it his brethren, and said, "Behold, I have dreamed a dream more; and, behold, the sun and the moon and the eleven stars made obeisance to me."

And he told it to his father and to his brethren; and his father rebuked him and said unto him, "What is this dream that thou hast dreamed? Shall I and thy mother and thy brethren indeed come to bow down ourselves to thee to the earth?" And his brethren envied him, but his father observed the saying. And his brethren went to feed their father's flock in Shechem.

And Israel said unto Joseph, "Do not thy brethren feed the flock in Shechem? Come, and I will send thee unto them."

And Joseph said to him, "Here am I."

And Israel said to him, "Go, I pray thee, see whether it be well with thy brethren and well with the flocks, and bring me word again." So he sent him out of the vale of Hebron and he came to Shechem.

And a certain man found him and, behold, he was wandering in the field; and the man asked him, saying, "What seekest thou?"

And Joseph said, "I seek my brethren; tell me, I pray thee, where they feed their flocks."

And the man said, "They are departed hence; for I heard them say, 'Let us go to Dothan.'"

And Joseph went after his brethren and found them in Dothan. And when they saw him afar off, even before he came near unto them, they conspired against him to slay him. And they said one to another:

"Behold, this dreamer cometh! Come now therefore, and let us slay him and cast him into some pit, and we will say, 'Some evil beast hath devoured him,' and we shall see what will become of his dreams."

And Reuben heard it and he delivered Joseph out of their hands and said, "Let us not kill him." And Reuben said unto them, "Shed no blood, but cast him into this pit that is in the wilderness, and lay no hand upon him," that he might rid him out of their hands, to deliver him to his father again.

And it came to pass when Joseph was come unto his brethren that they stripped Joseph out of his coat, his coat of many colours that was on him, and they took him and cast him into a pit; and the pit was empty, there was no water in it. And they sat down to eat bread; and they lifted up their eyes and looked and, behold, a company of Ishmeelites came from Gilead with their camels, bearing spicery and balm and myrrh, going to carry it down to Egypt.

And Judah said unto his brethren, "What profit is it if we slay our brother and conceal his blood? Come, and let us sell him to the Ishmeelites, and let not our hand be upon him, for he is our brother and our flesh."

And his brothers were content. And they drew and lifted up Joseph out of the pit and sold Joseph to the Ishmeelites for twenty pieces of silver; and they brought Joseph into Egypt.

And Reuben returned unto the pit, and, behold, Joseph was not in the pit, and he rent his clothes. And he returned unto his brethren and said:

"The child is not; and I, whither shall I go?"

And they took Joseph's coat, and killed a kid of the goats, and dipped the coat in the blood; and they sent the

coat of many colours and they brought it to their father and said, "This we have found. Know now whether it be thy son's coat or no?"

And he knew it and said, "It is my son's coat; an evil beast hath devoured him; Joseph is without doubt rent in pieces." And Jacob rent his clothes and put sackcloth upon his loins and mourned for his son many days. And all his sons and all his daughters rose to comfort him, but he refused to be comforted.

And he said, "For I will go down into the grave unto my son mourning." Thus his father wept for him.

Joseph Sold Into Egypt
GENESIS

The Ishmeelites sold Joseph into Egypt unto Potiphar, an officer of Pharaoh's, and captain of the guard. And Joseph found grace in his sight and he served him; and Potiphar made him overseer over his house and all that he had he put into his hand, and he knew not aught he had, save the bread which he did eat. And Joseph was a goodly person, and well favoured.

And it came to pass after these things that his master's wife cast her eyes upon Joseph, but he said unto his master's wife:

"Behold, my master wotteth not what is with me in the house, and he hath committed all that he hath to my hand. There is none greater in this house than I, neither hath he kept back any thing from me but thee, because thou art his wife. How then can I do this great wickedness and sin against God?"

And it came to pass, as she spake to Joseph day by day, that he hearkened not unto her. And it came to pass about this time that Joseph went into the house, and there was none of the men of the house there within. And she caught him by his garment, and he left his garment in her hand and fled, and got him out.

When she saw that he had left his garment in her hand, she called unto the men of her house, saying, "See, he hath brought in an Hebrew unto us to mock us; and when he heard that I lifted up my voice and cried, he left his garment with me and fled." And she laid up his garment by her, until his lord came home.

And she spake unto him, according to these words, saying, "The Hebrew servant, which thou hast brought unto us, came in to mock me. As I lifted up my voice and cried, he left his garment with me and fled out."

When his master heard the words of his wife, which she

spake unto him, his wrath was kindled. And Joseph's master took him and put him into the prison, a place where the king's prisoners were bound; but the Lord was with Joseph and shewed him mercy and gave him favour in the sight of the keeper of the prison. And the keeper of the prison committed to Joseph's hand all the prisoners that were in the prison; and whatsoever they did there, he was the doer of it.

After these things the butler of the king of Egypt and his baker had offended their lord, the king of Egypt. He put them in ward in the house of the captain of the guard, into the prison, the place where Joseph was bound.

And Joseph asked Pharaoh's officers that were with him in the ward of his lord's house, saying, "Wherefore look ye so sadly today?"

And they said unto him, "We have dreamed a dream, and there is no interpreter of it."

And Joseph said unto them, "Do not interpretations belong to God? Tell me them, I pray you." And the chief butler told his dream to Joseph.

And it came to pass the third day, which was Pharaoh's birthday, that he made a feast unto all his servants; and he lifted up the head of the chief butler and of the chief baker among his servants. And he restored the chief butler unto his butlership again; and he gave the cup into Pharaoh's hand, but he hanged the chief baker, as Joseph had interpreted to them.

Yet did not the chief butler remember Joseph, but forgat him.

And it came to pass at the end of two full years that Pharaoh dreamed. And, behold, he stood by the river. And, behold, there came up out of the river seven well favoured kine and fatfleshed, and they fed in a meadow. And behold, seven other kine came up after them out of the river, ill favoured and leanfleshed, and stood by the other kine upon the brink of the river. And the ill favoured and leanfleshed kine did eat up the seven well favoured and fat kine. So Pharaoh awoke.

And he slept and dreamed the second time. And, behold, seven ears of corn came up upon one stalk, rank and good. And, behold, seven thin ears and blasted with the east wind sprung up after them. And the seven thin ears devoured the seven rank and full ears. And Pharaoh awoke, and, behold, it was a dream.

And it came to pass in the morning that his spirit was troubled and he sent and called for all the magicians of Egypt and all the wise men thereof; and Pharaoh told them his dream, but there was none that could interpret them.

Then spake the chief butler unto Pharaoh, saying, "There was in prison with us a young man, an Hebrew, servant to the captain of the guard; and we told him, and he interpreted to us our dreams; to each man according to his dream he did interpret. As he interpreted to us, so it was; me he restored unto mine office, and the chief baker he hanged."

Then Pharaoh sent and called Joseph, and they brought him hastily out of the dungeon; and he shaved himself and changed his raiment, and came in unto Pharaoh.

And Pharaoh said unto Joseph, "I have dreamed a dream, and there is none that can interpret it; and I have heard say of thee that thou canst understand a dream to interpret it."

JOSEPH INTERPRETS PHAROAH'S DREAM

And Joseph answered Pharaoh, saying, "It is not in me: God shall give Pharaoh an answer of peace."

And Pharaoh said unto Joseph, "In my dream, behold, I stood upon the bank of the river. And I told this unto the magicians, but there was none that could declare it to me."

And Joseph said unto Pharaoh, "The dream of Pharaoh is one: God hath shewed Pharaoh what he is about to do. The seven good kine are seven years, and the seven good ears are seven years: the dream is one. And the seven thin and ill favoured kine that came up after them are seven years; and the seven empty ears blasted with the east wind shall be seven years of famine. Now therefore let Pharaoh look out a man discreet and wise, and set him over the land of Egypt. And let him appoint officers over the land. And let them gather all the food of those good years that come, and lay up corn under the hand of Pharaoh, and let them keep food in the cities. And that food shall be for store to the land against the seven years of famine which shall be in the land of Egypt, that the land perish not through the famine."

And Pharaoh said unto Joseph, "Forasmuch as God hath shewed thee all this, there is none so discreet and wise as thou art: thou shalt be over my house, and according unto thy word shall all my people be ruled. Only in the throne will I be greater than thou."

And Joseph was thirty years old when he stood before Pharaoh, king of Egypt. And Joseph went out from the presence of Pharaoh and went throughout all the land of Egypt. And in the seven plenteous years the earth brought forth by handfuls. And Joseph gathered corn as the sand of the sea, very much, until he left numbering, for it was without number.

And the seven years of dearth began to come, according as Joseph had said, and the dearth was in all lands, but in all the land of Egypt there was bread. And all countries came into Egypt to Joseph for to buy corn because that the famine was so sore in all lands.

Now Jacob said unto his sons, "Behold, I have heard that there is corn in Egypt; get you down thither and buy for us from thence, that we may live and not die."

And Joseph's ten brethren went down to buy corn in Egypt. But Benjamin, Joseph's brother, Jacob sent not with his brethren, for he said, "Lest peradventure mischief befall him."

And Joseph saw his brethren, and he knew them but made himself strange unto them and spake roughly unto them; and he said unto them, "Whence come ye?"

And they said, "From the land of Canaan to buy food."

And Joseph said unto them, "Ye are spies."

And they said unto him, "Nay, my lord, but to buy food are thy servants come!" And they said, "Thy servants are twelve brethren, the sons of one man in the land of Canaan; and, behold, the youngest is this day with our father, and one is not."

And Joseph said, "Hereby ye shall be proved: by the life of Pharaoh ye shall not go forth hence except your youngest brother come hither." And he put them all together into ward three days.

JOSEPH COMMANDS HIS BRETHREN

And Joseph said unto them the third day, "This do, and live, for I fear God. If ye be true men, let one of your brethren be bound in the house of your prison. Go ye, carry corn for the famine of your houses, but bring your youngest brother unto me: so shall your words be verified, and ye shall not die."

And they said one to another, "We are verily guilty concerning our brother, in that we saw the anguish of his soul, when he besought us, and we would not hear; therefore is this distress come upon us."

And Reuben answered them, saying, "Spake I not unto you, saying, 'Do not sin against the child,' and you would not hear? Therefore, behold, also his blood is required."

And they knew not that Joseph understood them, for he spake unto them by an interpreter. And he turned himself about from them and wept; and returned to them again and communed with them, and took from them Simeon and bound him before their eyes. Then Joseph commanded to fill their sacks with corn, and to restore every man's money into his sack, and to give them provision for the way; and thus did he unto them.

And they laded their asses with the corn and departed thence. And as one of them opened his sack to give his ass provender in the inn he espied his money, for, behold, it was in his sack's mouth.

And he said unto his brethren, "My money is restored, and, lo, it is even in my sack," and their heart failed them, and they were afraid, saying one to another, "What is this that God hath done unto us?"

And they came unto Jacob, their father, unto the land of Canaan, and told him all that befell unto them, saying, "The man who is the lord of the land spake roughly to us and took us for spies of the country. And the man said:

" 'Hereby shall I know that ye are true men: leave one of your brethren here with me and take food for the famine of your households and be gone; and bring your youngest brother unto me. Then shall I know that ye are no spies but that ye are true men. So will I deliver you your brother, and ye shall traffick in the land.' "

And it came to pass as they emptied their sacks that, behold, every man's bundle of money was in his sack; and when both they and their father saw the bundles of money they were afraid.

And Jacob, their father, said unto them, "Me have ye bereaved of my children; Joseph is not, and Simeon is not, and ye will take Benjamin away; all these things are against me."

And Reuben spake unto his father, saying, "Slay my two sons if I bring him not to thee; deliver him into my hand and I will bring him to thee again."

And Jacob said, "My son shall not go down with you, for his brother is dead and he is left alone; if mischief befall him by the way in the which ye go, then shall ye bring down my gray hairs with sorrow to the grave."

And the famine was sore in the land. And it came to pass, when they had eaten up the corn which they had brought out of Egypt, their father said unto them, "Go again, buy us a little food."

And Judah spake unto him, saying, "The man did solemnly protest unto us, saying, 'Ye shall not see my face except your brother be with you.' If thou wilt send our brother with us we will go down and buy thee food; but if thou wilt not send him we will not go down; for the man said unto us 'Ye shall not see my face, except your brother be with you.'"

And Israel said, "Wherefore dealt ye so ill with me as to tell the man whether ye had yet a brother?"

And they said, "The man asked us straitly of our state, and of our kindred, saying, 'Is your father yet alive? Have ye another brother?' And we told him according to the tenor of these words. Could we certainly know that he would say, 'Bring your brother down?'"

And Judah said unto Israel, his father, "Send the lad with me, and we will arise and go, that we may live, and not die, both we and thou, and also our little ones. I will be surety for him, of my hand shalt thou require him. If I bring him not unto thee and set him before thee, then let me bear the blame for ever. For except we had lingered, surely now we had returned this second time."

And their father Israel said unto them, "If it must be so now, do this. Take of the best fruits in the land in your vessels, and carry down the man a present, a little balm and a little honey, spices and myrrh, nuts and almonds. And take double money in your hand, and the money that was brought again in the mouth of your sacks, carry it again in your hand; peradventure it was an oversight. Take also your brother, and arise, go again unto the man. And God Almighty give you mercy before the man, that he may send away your other brother and Benjamin. If I be bereaved of my children I am bereaved."

And the men took that present, and they took double money in their hand, and Benjamin, and rose up and went down to Egypt and stood before Joseph.

And when Joseph saw Benjamin with them he said to the ruler of his house, "Bring these men home, and slay, and make ready, for these men shall dine with me at noon."

And the man did as Joseph bade; and the man brought the men into Joseph's house. And the men were afraid because they were brought into Joseph's house, and they said:

"Because of the money that was returned in our sacks at the first time are we brought in, that he may seek occasion against us and fall upon us and take us for bondmen, and our asses."

And they came near to the steward of Joseph's house, and they communed with him at the door of the house and said, "O sir, we came indeed down at the first time to buy food. And it came to pass, when we came to the inn, that we opened our sacks and, behold, every man's money was in the mouth of his sack, our money in full weight; and we have brought it again in our hand. And other money have we brought down in our hands to buy food; we cannot tell who put our money in our sacks."

And he said, "Peace be to you, fear not. Your God, and the God of your father, hath given you treasure in your sacks. I had your money." And he brought Simeon out unto them.

And the man brought the men into Joseph's house and gave them water and they washed their feet; and he gave their asses provender. And they made ready the present against Joseph came at noon, for they heard that they should eat bread there. And when Joseph came home they brought him the present which was in their hand into the house, and bowed themselves to him to the earth.

And he asked them of their welfare and said, "Is your father well, the old man of whom ye spake? Is he yet alive?"

And they answered, "Thy servant our father is in good health, he is yet alive." And they bowed down their heads and made obeisance.

And he lifted up his eyes and saw his brother Benjamin, his mother's son, and said, "Is this your younger brother, of whom ye spake unto me?" And he said, "God be gracious unto thee, my son."

Israel Comes to Egypt
GENESIS

And Joseph made haste, for his bowels did yearn upon his brother, and he sought where to weep; and he entered into his chamber and wept there. And he washed his face and went out and refrained himself and said, "Set on bread."

And they set on for him by himself, and for them by themselves, and for the Egyptians, which did eat with him, by themselves, because the Egyptians might not eat bread with the Hebrews, for that is an abomination unto the Egyptians. And they sat before him, the firstborn according to his birthright and the youngest according to his youth, and the men marvelled one at another. And he took and sent messes unto them from before him, but Benjamin's mess was five times so much as any of theirs. And they drank and were merry with him.

And he commanded the steward of his house, saying, "Fill the men's sacks with food, as much as they can carry, and put every man's money in his sack's mouth. And put my cup, the silver cup, in the sack's mouth of the youngest, and his corn money."

And he did according to the word that Joseph had spoken. As soon as the morning was light the men were sent away, they and their asses.

And when they were gone out of the city, and not yet far off, Joseph said unto his steward, "Up, follow after the men, and when thou dost overtake them say unto them, 'Wherefore have ye rewarded evil for good? Is not this it in which my lord drinketh, and whereby indeed he divineth? Ye have done evil in so doing.'" And he overtook them, and he spake unto them these same words.

And they said unto him, "Wherefore saith my lord these words? God forbid that thy servants should do according to this thing. Behold, the money which we found in our sacks' mouths we brought again unto thee out of the land of

Canaan; how then should we steal out of thy lord's house silver or gold? With whomsoever of thy servants it be found, both let him die and we also will be my lord's bondmen."

And he said, "Now also let it be according unto your words: he with whom it is found shall be my servant, and ye shall be blameless."

And they speedily took down every man his sack to the ground and opened every man his sack. And he searched, and began at the eldest and left at the youngest; and the cup was found in Benjamin's sack. Then they rent their clothes and laded every man his ass and returned to the city. And Judah and his brethren came to Joseph's house, for he was

yet there. And they fell before him on the ground.

And Joseph said unto them, "What deed is this that ye have done? Wot ye not that such a man as I can certainly divine?"

And Judah said, "What shall we say unto my lord? What shall we speak? Or how shall we clear ourselves? God hath found out the iniquity of thy servants: behold, we are my lord's servants, both we and he also with whom the cup is found."

And he said, "God forbid that I should do so; but the man in whose hand the cup is found, he shall be my servant, and as for you, get you up in peace unto your father."

Then Judah came near unto him and said, "Oh, my lord, let thy servant, I pray thee, speak! We have a father, an old man, and a child of his old age, a little one; and his brother is dead, and he alone is left of his mother, and his father loveth him. Now therefore when I come to thy servant, my father, and the lad be not with us, seeing that his life is bound up in the lad's life, it shall come to pass, when he seeth that the lad is not with us, that he will die; and thy servants shall bring down the gray hairs of thy servant, our father, with sorrow to the grave. Now therefore, I pray thee, let thy servant abide instead of the lad a bondman to my lord."

Then Joseph could not refrain himself before all them that stood by him, and he cried, "Cause every man to go out from me!" And there stood no man with him.

And Joseph said unto his brethren, "Come near to me, I pray you." And they came near. And he said, "I am Joseph, your brother, whom ye sold into Egypt. Now therefore be not grieved nor angry with yourselves that ye sold me hither, for God did send me before you to preserve life. Haste ye and go up to my father and say unto him, 'Thus saith thy son

Joseph: "Come down unto me." '" So he sent his brethren away, and they departed. And he said unto them, "See that ye fall not out by the way."

And they went up out of Egypt and came into the land of Canaan unto Jacob, their father, and told him, saying, "Joseph is yet alive, and he is governor over all the land of Egypt."

And Jacob's heart fainted, for he believed them not. And they told him all the words of Joseph which he had said unto them; and when he saw the wagons which Joseph had sent to carry him, the spirit of Jacob, their father, revived.

And Israel said, "It is enough. Joseph, my son, is yet alive. I will go and see him before I die."

And Israel took his journey with all that he had and came to Beersheba and offered sacrifices unto the God of his father, Isaac. And Jacob rose up from Beersheba, and the sons of Israel carried Jacob, their father, and their little ones and their wives, in the wagons which Pharaoh had sent to carry him. And they took their cattle and their goods, which they had gotten in the land of Canaan, and came into Egypt, Jacob and all his seed with him: his sons, and his sons' sons with him, his daughters, and his sons' daughters, and all his seed brought he with him into Egypt.

And he sent Judah before him unto Joseph, to direct his face unto Goshen. And they came into the land of Goshen. And Joseph made ready his chariot and went up to meet Israel, his father, to Goshen, and presented himself unto him, and he fell on his neck and wept on his neck a good while.

And Israel said unto Joseph, "Now let me die, since I have seen thy face, because thou art yet alive."

And Joseph dwelt in Egypt, he and his father's house. And Joseph lived an hundred and ten years. And Joseph died, and all his brethren, and all that generation.

THE BIRTH OF ISRAEL

Now there arose up a new king over Egypt, which knew not Joseph. And he said unto his people, "Behold, the people of the children of Israel are more and mightier than we. Come on, let us deal wisely with them lest they multiply and it come to pass that, when there falleth out any war, they join also unto our enemies and fight against us and so get them up out of the land."

*Moses
In the
Bulrushes*
EXODUS
78
Therefore they did set over them taskmasters to afflict them with their burdens. And they built for Pharaoh treasure cities, Pithom and Raamses. But the more they afflicted them the more they multiplied and grew. And the Egyptians made their lives bitter with hard bondage, in mortar and in brick and in all manner of service in the field.

And Pharaoh charged all his people, saying, "Every son that is born of the Hebrews ye shall cast into the river, and every daughter ye shall save alive."

And there went a man of the house of Levi and took to wife a daughter of Levi. And the woman bare a son, and when she saw him that he was a goodly child, she hid him three months. And when she could not longer hide him she took for him an ark of bulrushes and daubed it with slime and with pitch, and put the child therein; and she laid it in the flags by the river's brink. And his sister stood afar off, to wit what would be done to him. And the daughter of Pharaoh came down to wash herself at the river, and her maidens

Moses
In the
Bulrushes
EXODUS

walked along by the river's side; and when she saw the ark among the flags she sent her maid to fetch it. And when she had opened it she saw the child and, behold, the babe wept.

And she had compassion on him and said, "This is one of the Hebrews' children."

Then said his sister to Pharaoh's daughter, "Shall I go and call to thee a nurse of the Hebrew women, that she may nurse the child for thee?"

And Pharaoh's daughter said to her, "Go!" And the maid went and called the child's mother.

And Pharaoh's daughter said unto her, "Take this child away and nurse it for me, and I will give thee thy wages." And the woman took the child and nursed it.

And the child grew, and she brought him unto Pharaoh's daughter and he became her son. And she called his name Moses: and she said, "Because I drew him out of the water."

And it came to pass in those days, when Moses was grown, that he went out unto his brethren and looked on their burdens; and he spied an Egyptian smiting an Hebrew, one of his brethren. And he looked this way and that way, and when he saw that there was no man he slew the Egyptian and hid him in the sand.

And when he went out the second day, behold, two men of the Hebrews strove together, and Moses said to him that did the wrong, "Wherefore smitest thou thy fellow?"

And he said, "Who made thee a prince and a judge over us? Intendest thou to kill me, as thou killedst the Egyptian?"

And Moses feared, and said, "Surely this thing is known."

Now when Pharaoh heard this thing he sought to slay Moses. But Moses fled from the face of Pharaoh and dwelt in the land of Midian.

Now Moses kept the flock of Jethro, his father-in-law, the priest of Midian; and he led the flock to the backside of the desert and came to the mountain of God, even to Horeb. And the angel of the Lord appeared unto him in a flame of fire out of the midst of a bush; and Moses looked and, behold, the bush burned with fire and the bush was not consumed.

And Moses said, "I will now turn aside and see this great sight, why the bush is not burnt."

And when the Lord saw that he turned aside to see, God called unto him out of the midst of the bush and said, "Moses, Moses!"

And he said, "Here am I!"

And the Lord said, "Draw not nigh hither; put off thy shoes from off thy feet, for the place whereon thou standest is holy ground." Moreover he said, "I am the God of thy father, the God of Abraham, the God of Isaac, and the God of Jacob."

And Moses hid his face, for he was afraid to look upon God.

And the Lord said, "I have surely seen the affliction of my people which are in Egypt, and have heard their cry by reason of their taskmasters, for I know their sorrows. And I am come down to deliver them out of the hand of the Egyptians and to bring them up out of that land unto a good land and a large, unto a land flowing with milk and honey. Come now therefore and I will send thee unto Pharaoh that thou mayest bring forth my people out of Egypt."

And Moses said unto God, "Who am I that I should go

unto Pharaoh and that I should bring forth the children of Israel out of Egypt?"

And the Lord said, "Certainly I will be with thee, and this shall be a token unto thee."

And Moses answered and said, "But, behold, they will not believe me, nor hearken unto my voice, for they will say, 'The Lord hath not appeared unto thee.'"

And the Lord said unto him, "What is that in thine hand?"

And he said, "A rod."

And the Lord said, "Cast it on the ground." And he cast

it on the ground and it became a serpent, and Moses fled from before it.

And the Lord said unto Moses, "Put forth thine hand and take it by the tail." And he put forth his hand and caught it, and it became a rod in his hand.

And the Lord said furthermore unto him, "Put now thine hand into thy bosom." And Moses put his hand into his bosom, and when he took it out, behold, his hand was leprous as snow.

And the Lord said, "Put thine hand into thy bosom again." And he put his hand into his bosom again, and plucked it out of his bosom, and, behold, it was turned again as his other flesh.

"And it shall come to pass, if they will not believe thee, neither hearken to the voice of the first sign, that they will believe the voice of the latter sign."

And Moses said unto the Lord, "O my Lord, I am not eloquent, neither heretofore, nor since thou hast spoken unto thy servant, but I am slow of speech and of a slow tongue."

And the Lord said unto him, "Now therefore go, and I will be with thy mouth and teach thee what thou shalt say. Is not Aaron, the Levite, thy brother? I know that he can speak well. And also, behold, he cometh forth to meet thee, and when he seeth thee he will be glad in his heart. And thou shalt speak unto him and put words in his mouth. And I will be with thy mouth and with his mouth and will teach you what ye shall do."

And Moses went and returned to Jethro, his father-in-law, and said unto him, "Let me go, I pray thee, and return unto my brethren which are in Egypt and see whether they be yet alive."

And Jethro said to Moses, "Go in peace."

And the Lord said to Aaron, "Go into the wilderness to meet Moses."

And Aaron went and met Moses in the mount of God and kissed him. And Moses told Aaron all the words of the Lord who had sent him, and all the signs which he had commanded him.

And Moses and Aaron went and gathered together all the elders of the children of Israel; and Aaron spake all the words which the Lord had spoken unto Moses and did the signs in the sight of the people. And the people believed, and when they heard that the Lord had visited the children of Israel and that he had looked upon their affliction, then they bowed their heads and worshipped.

And the Lord hardened Pharaoh's heart, that he hearkened not unto them, as the Lord had said.

And the Lord said unto Moses, "Get thee unto Pharaoh. And thou shalt say unto him, 'Thus saith the Lord: "In this thou shalt know that I am the Lord: behold, I will smite with the rod that is in mine hand upon the waters which are in the river, and they shall be turned to blood. And the fish that is in the river shall die; and the river shall stink, and the Egyptians shall loathe to drink of the water of the river."'"

And Moses and Aaron did so, as the Lord commanded. And all the waters that were in the river were turned to blood.

And the Lord spake unto Moses. "Go unto Pharaoh and say unto him, 'Thus saith the Lord: "Let my people go, that they may serve me. And if thou refuse to let them go, behold, I will smite all thy borders with frogs."'"

And the Lord spake unto Moses. "Say unto Aaron, 'Stretch forth thine hand with thy rod over the streams, over the rivers, and over the ponds, and cause frogs to come up upon the land of Egypt.'" And Aaron stretched out his hand over the waters of Egypt, and the frogs came up and

THE PLAGUE OF FROGS

covered the land of Egypt.

Then Pharaoh called for Moses and Aaron and said, "Entreat the Lord that he may take away the frogs from me and from my people, and I will let the people go."

And Moses and Aaron went out from Pharaoh; and Moses cried unto the Lord because of the frogs which he had brought against Pharaoh. And the Lord did according to the word of Moses, and the frogs died out of the houses, out of the villages, and out of the fields. And they gathered them together upon heaps, and the land stank. But when Pharaoh saw that there was respite he hardened his heart and hearkened not unto them, as the Lord had said.

And the Lord said unto Moses, "Say unto Aaron, 'Stretch out thy rod and smite the dust of the land, that it may became lice throughout all the land of Egypt.'"

And they did so; for Aaron stretched out his hand with his rod and smote the dust of the earth, and it became lice in man and in beast; all the dust of the land became lice throughout all the land of Egypt.

And the Lord said unto Moses, "Rise up early in the morning and stand before Pharaoh; lo, he cometh forth to the water; and say unto him, 'Thus saith the Lord: "Let my people go, else, if thou wilt not let my people go, behold, I will send swarms of flies upon thee and upon thy servants and upon thy people and into thy houses; and the houses of the Egyptians shall be full of swarms of flies, and also the ground whereon they are."'"

And the Lord did so, and there came a grievous swarm of flies into the house of Pharaoh and into his servants' houses and into all the land of Egypt. The land was corrupted by reason of the swarm of flies.

And Pharaoh called for Moses and for Aaron and said, "Go ye!"

And Moses went out from Pharaoh and entreated the Lord. And the Lord did according to the word of Moses, and he removed the swarms of flies from Pharaoh, from his servants, and from his people; there remained not one. And Pharaoh hardened his heart at this time also, neither would he let the people go.

Then the Lord said unto Moses, "Go in unto Pharaoh and tell him, 'Thus saith the Lord God of the Hebrews: "Let my people go, for if thou refuse to let them go and wilt hold them still, behold, the hand of the Lord is upon thy cattle which is in the field, upon the horses, upon the asses, upon the camels, upon the oxen, and upon the sheep; there shall be a very grievous murrain."'"

And the Lord did that thing on the morrow, and all the cattle of Egypt died, but of the cattle of the children of Israel died not one. And Pharaoh sent, and, behold, there was not one of the cattle of the Israelites dead. And the heart of Pharaoh was hardened and he did not let the people go.

And the Lord said unto Moses and unto Aaron, "Take to you handfuls of ashes of the furnace and let Moses sprinkle it toward the heaven in the sight of Pharaoh. And it shall become small dust in all the land of Egypt, and shall be a boil breaking forth with blains upon man and upon beast throughout all the land of Egypt."

And they took ashes of the furnace and stood before Pharaoh; and Moses sprinkled it up toward heaven, and it became a boil breaking forth with blains upon man and upon beast. And the Lord hardened the heart of Pharaoh and he hearkened not unto them, as the Lord had spoken unto Moses.

And the Lord said unto Moses, "Rise up early in the morning and stand before Pharaoh and say unto him, 'Thus saith the Lord God of the Hebrews: "Let my people go;

THE PLAGUE OF RAIN AND HAIL

behold, tomorrow about this time I will cause it to rain a very grievous hail, such as hath not been in Egypt since the foundation thereof even until now.' " "

And Moses stretched forth his rod toward heaven, and the Lord sent thunder and hail, and the fire ran along upon the ground; and the Lord rained hail upon the land of Egypt. Only in the land of Goshen, where the children of Israel were, was there no hail.

And Pharaoh sent and called for Moses and Aaron and said unto them, "I have sinned this time; the Lord is righteous, and I and my people are wicked. Entreat the Lord (for it is enough) that there be no more mighty thunderings and hail; and I will let you go, and ye shall stay no longer."

And Moses went out of the city from Pharaoh and spread abroad his hands unto the Lord; and the thunders and hail ceased, and the rain was not poured upon the earth. And the heart of Pharaoh was hardened, neither would he let the children of Israel go, as the Lord had spoken by Moses.

And Moses and Aaron came in unto Pharaoh and said unto him, "Thus saith the Lord God of the Hebrews: 'How long wilt thou refuse to humble thyself before me? Let my people go, that they may serve me. Else, if thou refuse to let my people go, behold, tomorrow will I bring the locusts into thy coast, and they shall cover the face of the earth, that one cannot be able to see the earth.' "

And Moses stretched forth his rod over the land of Egypt, and the Lord brought an east wind upon the land all that day and all that night; and when it was morning the east wind brought the locusts. And they did eat every herb of the land and all the fruit of the trees which the hail had left, and there remained not any green thing in the trees or in the herbs of the field, through all the land of Egypt.

Then Pharaoh called for Moses and Aaron in haste,

and he said, "I have sinned against the Lord, your God, and against you."

And the Lord turned a mighty strong west wind which took away the locusts and cast them into the Red Sea. But the Lord hardened Pharaoh's heart so that he would not let the children of Israel go.

And the Lord said unto Moses, "Stretch out thine hand toward heaven, that there may be darkness over the land of Egypt, even darkness which may be felt." And Moses stretched forth his hand toward heaven; and there was a thick darkness in all the land of Egypt three days.

And Pharaoh called unto Moses and said, "Go ye, serve the Lord. Only let your flocks and your herds be stayed; let your little ones also go with you."

And Moses said, "Our cattle also shall go with us; there shall not an hoof be left behind." But the Lord hardened Pharaoh's heart and he would not let them go.

And Pharaoh said unto him, "Get thee from me, take heed to thyself, see my face no more, for in that day thou seest my face thou shalt die."

And Moses said, "Thou hast spoken well. I will see thy face again no more."

And the Lord said unto Moses, "Yet will I bring one plague more upon Pharaoh and upon Egypt; afterwards he will let you go hence."

Then Moses called for all the elders of Israel and said unto them, "Draw out and take you a lamb according to your families, and kill the passover. And ye shall take a bunch of hyssop and dip it in the blood that is in the basin, and strike the lintel and the two side posts with the blood that is in the basin. And none of you shall go out at the door of his house until the morning, for the Lord will pass through to smite the Egyptians; and when he seeth the blood upon the lintel and on the two side posts, the Lord will pass over the door and will not suffer the destroyer to come in unto your houses to smite you.

"And ye shall observe this thing for an ordinance to thee and to thy sons for ever. And it shall come to pass, when your children shall say unto you, 'What mean ye by this service?' that ye shall say, 'It is the sacrifice of the Lord's passover, who passed over the houses of the children of Israel in Egypt, when he smote the Egyptians and delivered our houses.' And the people bowed the head and worshipped."

And the children of Israel went away and did as the Lord had commanded. And it came to pass that at midnight the Lord smote all the firstborn in the land of Egypt, from the firstborn of Pharaoh that sat on his throne unto the firstborn of the captive that was in the dungeon; and all the firstborn of cattle. And Pharaoh rose up in the night, he and all his servants and all the Egyptians, and there was a great cry in Egypt, for there was not a house where there was not one dead.

And he called for Moses and Aaron by night and said, "Rise up and get you forth from among my people, both ye and the children of Israel; and go, serve the Lord, as ye have said. Also take your flocks and your herds, as ye have said, and be gone; and bless me also."

And the Egyptians were urgent upon the people, that they might send them out of the land in haste, for they said, "We be all dead men."

And the people took their dough before it was leavened, their kneadingtroughs being bound up in their clothes upon their shoulders.

And the Lord went before them by day in a pillar of a
cloud, to lead them the way, and by night in a pillar of fire,
to give them light, to go by day and night.

And it was told the king of Egypt that the people fled;

and the heart of Pharaoh and of his servants was turned against the people, and they said, "Why have we done this, that we have let Israel go from serving us?"

And the Lord hardened the heart of Pharaoh, king of Egypt, and he pursued after the children of Israel. And when Pharaoh drew nigh, the children of Israel lifted up their eyes, and, behold, the Egyptians marched after them, and they were sore afraid; and the children of Israel cried out unto the Lord.

And they said unto Moses, "Because there were no graves in Egypt, hast thou taken us away to die in the wilderness? Wherefore hast thou dealt thus with us, to carry us forth out of Egypt? Is not this the word that we did tell thee in Egypt, saying, 'Let us alone, that we may serve the Egyptians'? For it had been better for us to serve the Egyptians than that we should die in the wilderness."

And Moses said unto the people, "Fear ye not, stand still and see the salvation of the Lord, which he will shew to you today."

And Moses stretched out his hand over the sea, and the Lord caused the sea to go back by a strong east wind all that night, and made the sea dry land, and the waters were divided. And the children of Israel went into the midst of the sea upon the dry ground.

And the Egyptians pursued and went in after them to the midst of the sea, even all Pharaoh's horses, his chariots, and his horsemen. And Moses stretched forth his hand over the sea, and the sea returned to his strength when the morning appeared; and the Egyptians fled against it. And the Lord overthrew the Egyptians in the midst of the sea. And the waters returned and covered the chariots and the horsemen and all the host of Pharaoh that came into the sea after them; there remained not so much as one of them.

So Moses brought Israel from the Red Sea, and they went out into the wilderness of Shur; and they went three days in the wilderness and found no water. And when they came to Marah they could not drink of the waters of Marah, for they were bitter; therefore the name of it was called Marah.

And the people murmured against Moses, saying, "What shall we drink?"

And he cried unto the Lord; and the Lord shewed him a tree, which, when he had cast into the waters, the waters were made sweet.

And the whole congregation of the children of Israel murmured against Moses and Aaron in the wilderness. And the children of Israel said unto them, "Would to God we had died by the hand of the Lord in the land of Egypt, when we sat by the flesh pots and when we did eat bread to the full, for ye have brought us forth into this wilderness to kill this whole assembly with hunger."

Then said the Lord unto Moses, "Behold, I will rain bread from heaven for you."

And it came to pass that at even the quails came up and

covered the camp, and in the morning the dew lay round about the host. And when the dew that lay was gone up, behold, upon the face of the wilderness there lay a small round thing, as small as the hoar frost on the ground.

And when the children of Israel saw it they said one to another, "It is manna," for they wist not what it was.

And Moses said unto them, "This is the bread which the Lord hath given you to eat."

And the house of Israel called the name thereof manna; and it was like coriander seed, white, and the taste of it was like wafers made with honey.

And there was no water for the people to drink. Wherefore the people did chide with Moses and said, "Give us water that we may drink!"

And Moses said unto them, "Why chide ye with me? Wherefore do ye tempt the Lord?"

And the people thirsted there for water; and the people murmured against Moses and said, "Wherefore is this that thou hast brought us up out of Egypt, to kill us and our children and our cattle with thirst?"

And Moses cried unto the Lord, saying, "What shall I do unto this people? They be almost ready to stone me."

And the Lord said unto Moses, "Go on before the people and take with thee of the elders of Israel; and thy rod, wherewith thou smotest the river, take in thine hand and go. Behold, I will stand before thee there upon the rock in Horeb; and thou shalt smite the rock, and there shall come water out of it that the people may drink."

And Moses did so in the sight of the elders of Israel. And he called the name of the place Massah, and Meribah, because of the chiding of the children of Israel, and because they tempted the Lord, saying, "Is the Lord among us or not?"

THE CHILDREN OF ISRAEL GATHER MANNA

In the third month, when the children of Israel were gone forth out of the land of Egypt, the same day came they into the wilderness of Sinai. And there Israel camped before the mount.

And Moses went up unto God, and the Lord called unto him out of the mountain, saying, "Thus shalt thou say to the house of Jacob and tell the children of Israel: 'Ye have seen what I did unto the Egyptians, and how I bare you on eagles' wings and brought you unto myself. Now therefore, if ye will obey my voice indeed and keep my covenant, then ye shall be a peculiar treasure unto me above all people, for all the earth is mine. And ye shall be unto me a kingdom of priests and an holy nation.' These are the words which thou shalt speak unto the children of Israel."

And Moses came and called for the elders of the people and laid before their faces all these words which the Lord commanded him. And all the people answered together, and said, "All that the Lord hath spoken we will do."

And the Lord said unto Moses, "Go unto the people and sanctify them today and tomorrow, and let them wash their clothes."

And Moses went down from the mount unto the people and sanctified the people, and they washed their clothes. And he said unto the people, "Be ready against the third day."

And the Lord called Moses up to the top of the mount, and Moses went up. And God spake all these words, saying, "I am the Lord, thy God, which have brought thee out of the land of Egypt, out of the house of bondage."

Thou shalt have no other gods before me.

"Thou shalt not make unto thee any graven image, or any likeness of any thing that is in heaven above, or that is in the earth beneath, or that is in the water under the earth. Thou shalt not bow down thyself to them nor serve them: for I, the Lord, thy God, am a jealous God, visiting the iniquity of the fathers upon the children unto the third and fourth generation of them that hate me, and shewing mercy unto thousands of them that love me and keep my commandments.

"Thou shalt not take the name of the Lord thy God in vain, for the Lord will not hold him guiltless that taketh his name in vain.

"Remember the Sabbath day, to keep it holy. Six days shalt thou labour and do all thy work, but the seventh day is the Sabbath of the Lord, thy God; in it thou shalt not do any work, thou, nor thy son, nor thy daughter, thy manservant nor thy maidservant, nor thy cattle, nor thy stranger that is within thy gates; for in six days the Lord made heaven and earth, the sea, and all that in them is, and rested the seventh day. Wherefore the Lord blessed the Sabbath day and hallowed it.

"Honour thy father and thy mother, that thy days may be long upon the land which the Lord, thy God, giveth thee.

"Thou shalt not kill.

"Thou shalt not commit adultery.

"Thou shalt not steal.

"Thou shalt not bear false witness against thy neighbour.

"Thou shalt not covet thy neighbour's house, thou shalt not covet thy neighbour's wife, nor his manservant, nor his maidservant, nor his ox, nor his ass, nor anything that is thy neighbour's."

MOSES SEES THE GOLDEN CALF

And all the people saw the thunderings and the lightnings, and the noise of the trumpet, and the mountain smoking; and when the people saw it they removed and stood afar off.

And the Lord said unto Moses, "Come up to me into the mount and be there, and I will give thee tables of stone, and a law, and commandments which I have written, that thou mayest teach them."

And Moses rose up, and his minister Joshua. And he said unto the elders, "Tarry ye here for us, until we come again unto you, and, behold, Aaron and Hur are with you. If any man have any matters to do, let him come unto them."

And Moses went up into the mount, and a cloud covered the mount. And Moses went into the midst of the cloud and gat him up into the mount. And Moses was in the mount forty days and forty nights.

And when the people saw that Moses delayed to come down out of the mount the people gathered themselves together unto Aaron and said unto him, "Up, make us gods which shall go before us; for as for this Moses, the man that brought us up out of the land of Egypt, we wot not what is become of him."

And Aaron said unto them, "Break off the golden earrings which are in the ears of your wives, of your sons, and of your daughters, and bring them unto me."

And all the people brake off the golden earrings which were in their ears and brought them unto Aaron. And he received them at their hand and fashioned it with a graving tool, after he had made it a molten calf.

And they said, "These be thy gods, O Israel, which brought thee up out of the land of Egypt."

And when Aaron saw it he built an altar before it; and

Aaron made proclamation and said, "Tomorrow is a feast to the Lord."

And they rose up early on the morrow and offered burnt offerings and brought peace offerings; and the people sat down to eat and to drink, and rose up to play.

And the Lord said unto Moses, "Go, get thee down; for thy people, which thou broughtest out of the land of Egypt, have corrupted themselves."

And Moses turned and went down from the mount, and the two tables of the testimony were in his hand. The tables were written on both their sides, on the one side and on the other were they written.

And it came to pass, as soon as he came nigh unto the camp, that he saw the calf and the dancing. And Moses' anger waxed hot, and he cast the tables out of his hands and brake them beneath the mount. And he took the calf which they had made and burnt it in the fire, and ground it to powder and strawed it upon the water, and made the children of Israel drink of it.

Then Moses stood in the gate of the camp and said, "Who is on the Lord's side? Let him come unto me." And all the sons of Levi gathered themselves together unto him.

And he said unto them, "Thus saith the Lord God of Israel, 'Put every man his sword by his side and go in and out from gate to gate throughout the camp and slay every man his brother, and every man his companion, and every man his neighbour.'" And the children of Levi did according to the word of Moses. And there fell of the people that day about three thousand men.

And it came to pass on the morrow that Moses said unto the people, "Ye have sinned a great sin; and now I will go up unto the Lord, peradventure I shall make an atonement for your sin."

BRINGING THE FRUIT FROM CANAAN

And the Lord spake unto Moses, saying, "Send thou men, that they may search the land of Canaan which I give unto the children of Israel. Of every tribe of their fathers shall ye send a man, every one a ruler among them."

And Moses sent them to spy out the land of Canaan and said unto them, "Get you up this way southward, and go up into the mountain and see the land, what it is, and the people that dwelleth therein, whether they be strong or weak, few or many. And what the land is that they dwell in, whether it be good or bad, and what cities they be that they dwell in, whether in tents or in strong holds. And what the land is, whether it be fat or lean, whether there be wood therein or not. And be ye of good courage, and bring of the fruit of the land."

Now the time was the time of the firstripe grapes. And they came unto the brook of Eshcol and cut down from thence a branch with one cluster of grapes, and they bare it between two upon a staff, and they brought of the pomegranates and of the figs.

And they went and came to Moses and to Aaron and to all the congregation of the children of Israel and said, "We came unto the land whither thou sentest us, and surely it floweth with milk and honey, and this is the fruit of it. Nevertheless, the people be strong that dwell in the land, and the cities are walled and very great."

And all the congregation lifted up their voice and cried and the people wept that night.

And all the children of Israel murmured against Moses and against Aaron, and the whole congregation said unto them, "Would God that we had died in the land of Egypt or would God we had died in this wilderness!"

And the Lord said unto Moses, "How long will this people provoke me and how long will it be ere they believe me, for all the signs which I have shewed among them? I will smite them with the pestilence and disinherit them, and will make of thee a greater nation and mightier than they."

And Moses said unto the Lord, "Pardon, I beseech thee, the iniquity of this people according unto the greatness of thy mercy, and as thou hast forgiven this people, from Egypt even until now."

And the Lord said, "I have pardoned according to thy word, but as truly as I live, all the earth shall be filled with the glory of the Lord. Say unto them, ' "As truly as I live," saith the Lord, "as ye have spoken in mine ears, so will I do to you. Your carcases shall fall in this wilderness and all that were numbered of you, according to your whole number, from twenty years old and upward, which have murmured against me, doubtless ye shall not come into the land, concerning which I sware to make you dwell therein, save Caleb, the son of Jephunneh, and Joshua, the son of Nun. But as for you, your carcases, they shall fall in this wilderness. And your children shall wander in the wilderness forty years." ' "

And the Lord spake unto Moses, saying, "Get thee up into this mountain Abarim, unto Mount Nebo, which is in the land of Moab, that is over against Jericho; and behold the land of Canaan, which I give unto the children of Israel for a possession."

And Moses went up from the plains of Moab unto the mountain of Nebo, to the top of Pisgah, that is over against Jericho. And the Lord shewed him all the land of Gilead, unto Dan, and all Naphtali, and the land of Ephraim, and Manasseh, and all the land of Judah, unto the utmost sea; and the south, and the plain of the valley of Jericho, the city of palm trees, unto Zoar.

And the Lord said unto him, "This is the land which I sware unto Abraham, unto Isaac, and unto Jacob, saying, 'I will give it unto thy seed.' I have caused thee to see it with thine eyes, but thou shalt not go over thither."

So Moses, the servant of the Lord, died there in the land of Moab, according to the word of the Lord. And he buried him in a valley in the land of Moab, over against Beth-peor, but no man knoweth of his sepulchre unto this day. And Moses was an hundred and twenty years old when he died. His eye was not dim nor his natural force abated. And the children of Israel wept for Moses in the plains of Moab thirty days. So the days of weeping and mourning for Moses were ended.

Moses Dies
DEUTERONOMY

And Joshua, the son of Nun, was full of the spirit of wisdom, for Moses had laid his hands upon him. And the children of Israel hearkened unto him and did as the Lord commanded Moses.

ow after the death of Moses, the servant of the Lord, it came to pass that the Lord spake unto Joshua, the son of Nun, Moses' minister, saying:

"Moses, my servant, is dead; now therefore arise, go over this Jordan, thou and all this people, unto the land which I do give to them, even to the children of Israel."

And Joshua rose early in the morning and came to Jordan, he and all the children of Israel, and lodged there before they passed over.

And Joshua said unto the people, "Sanctify yourselves, for tomorrow the Lord will do wonders among you."

And Joshua spake unto the priests, saying, "Take up the ark of the covenant and pass over before the people." And they took up the ark of the covenant and went before the people.

And it came to pass, when the people removed from their tents to pass over Jordan, and the priests bearing the ark of the covenant before the people, and as they that bare the ark were come unto Jordan, and the feet of the priests that bare the ark were dipped in the brim of the water (for

Jordan overfloweth all his banks all the time of harvest), that the waters which came down from above stood and rose up upon an heap very far from the city Adam that is beside Zaretan; and those that came down toward the sea of the plain, even the salt sea, failed and were cut off; and the people passed over right against Jericho. And the priests that bare the ark of the covenant of the Lord stood firm on dry ground in the midst of Jordan, and all the Israelites passed over on dry ground, until all the people were passed clean over Jordan.

Now Jericho was straitly shut up because of the children of Israel. None went out and none came in. And it came to pass on the seventh day that they rose early about the dawning of the day and compassed the city seven times. And it came to pass at the seventh time, when the priests blew with the trumpets, Joshua said unto the people, "Shout, for the Lord hath given you the city!"

So the people shouted when the priests blew with the trumpets, and it came to pass, when the people heard the sound of the trumpet, and the people shouted with a great shout, that the wall fell down flat, so that the people went up into the city, every man straight before him, and they took the city.

The children of Israel did evil in the sight of the Lord, and the Lord sold them into the hand of Jabin, king of Canaan, that reigned in Hazor; the captain of whose host was Sisera, which dwelt in Harosheth of the Gentiles. And the children of Israel cried unto the Lord, for he had nine hundred chariots of iron, and twenty years he mightily oppressed the children of Israel.

And Deborah, a prophetess, the wife of Lapidoth, she judged Israel at that time. And she dwelt under the palm tree of Deborah between Ramah and Bethel in Mount Ephraim; and the children of Israel came up to her for judgment.

And she sent and called Barak and said unto him, "Hath not the Lord God of Israel commanded, saying, 'Go and draw toward Mount Tabor and take with thee ten thousand men of the children of Naphtali and of the children of Zebulun. And I will draw unto thee, to the river Kishon, Sisera, the captain of Jabin's army, with his chariots and his multitude; and I will deliver him into thine hand'?"

And Barak said unto her, "If thou wilt go with me, then I will go; but if thou wilt not go with me, then I will not go."

And she said, "I will surely go with thee, notwithstanding the journey that thou takest shall not be for thine honour, for the Lord shall sell Sisera into the hand of a woman."

And Deborah arose and went with Barak to Kedesh. And Barak called Zebulun and Naphtali to Kedesh, and he went up with ten thousand men at his feet; and Deborah went up with him.

Now Heber the Kenite, which was of the children of Hobab, the father-in-law of Moses, had severed himself from the Kenites and pitched his tent unto the plain of Zaanaim, which is by Kedesh.

And they shewed Sisera that Barak was gone up to Mount Tabor. And Sisera gathered together all his chariots, even nine hundred chariots of iron, and all the people that were with him.

And Deborah said unto Barak, "Up, for this is the day in which the Lord hath delivered Sisera into thine hand. Is not the Lord gone out before thee?"

So Barak went down from Mount Tabor, and ten thousand men after him. And the Lord discomfited Sisera, and all his chariots, and all his host, with the edge of the sword before Barak, so that Sisera lighted down off his chariot and fled away on his feet. But Barak pursued after the chariots and after the host, unto Harosheth of the Gentiles. And all the host of Sisera fell upon the edge of the sword and there was not a man left. Howbeit Sisera fled away on his feet to the tent of Jael, the wife of Heber the Kenite; for there was peace between Jabin, the king of Hazor, and the house of Heber the Kenite.

And Jael went out to meet Sisera and said unto him, "Turn in, my lord, turn in to me. Fear not." And when he had turned in unto her into the tent, she covered him with a mantle.

And he said unto her, "Give me, I pray thee, a little water to drink, for I am thirsty." And she opened a bottle of milk and gave him drink, and covered him.

Again he said unto her, "Stand in the door of the tent, and it shall be, when any man doth come and inquire of thee, and say, 'is there any man here?' that thou shalt say, 'No.'"

Then Jael, Heber's wife, took a nail of the tent, and took

an hammer in her hand, and went softly unto him and smote the nail into his temples and fastened it into the ground, for he was fast asleep and weary. So he died.

And, behold, as Barak pursued Sisera, Jael came out to meet him and said unto him, "Come, and I will shew thee the man whom thou seekest."

And when he came into her tent, behold, Sisera lay dead, and the nail was in his temples.

And the children of Israel did evil in the sight of the Lord, and the Lord delivered them into the hand of Midian seven years. And the hand of Midian prevailed against Israel. And because of the Midianites the children of Israel made them the dens which are in the mountains, and caves, and strong holds.

And there came an angel of the Lord and sat under an oak which was in Ophrah, that pertained unto Joash the Abiezrite; and his son Gideon threshed wheat by the wine-press, to hide it from the Midianites.

And the angel of the Lord appeared unto him and said unto him, "The Lord is with thee, thou mighty man of valour."

And Gideon said unto him, "Oh my Lord, if the Lord be with us, why then is all this befallen us? And where be all his miracles which our fathers told us of, saying, 'Did not the Lord bring us up from Egypt?' But now the Lord hath forsaken us and delivered us into the hands of the Midianites."

And the Lord looked upon him and said, "Go in this thy might, and thou shalt save Israel from the hand of the Midianites. Have not I sent thee?"

And Gideon said unto him, "Oh my Lord, wherewith shall I save Israel? Behold, my family is poor in Manasseh, and I am the least in my father's house."

And the Lord said unto him, "Surely I will be with thee, and thou shalt smite the Midianites as one man."

And Gideon said unto him, "If now I have found grace in thy sight, then shew me a sign that thou talkest with me." And Gideon said unto God, "If thou wilt save Israel by mine hand, as thou hast said, behold, I will put a fleece of wool in the floor; and if the dew be on the fleece only, and it be dry upon all the earth beside, then shall I know that thou wilt save Israel by mine hand, as thou hast said."

And it was so, for he rose up early on the morrow and thrust the fleece together and wringed the dew out of the fleece, a bowl full of water.

Then Gideon, and all the people that were with him, rose up early and pitched beside the well of Harod, so that the host of the Midianites were on the north side of them, by the hill of Moreh, in the valley.

And the Lord said unto Gideon, "The people that are with thee are too many for me to give the Midianites into their hands, lest Israel vaunt themselves against me, saying, 'Mine own hand hath saved me.' Now therefore go to, proclaim in the ears of the people, saying, 'Whosoever is fearful and afraid, let him return and depart early from Mount Gilead.'" And there returned of the people twenty and two thousand; and there remained ten thousand.

And the Lord said unto Gideon, "The people are yet too many; bring them down unto the water and I will try them for thee there."

So he brought down the people unto the water, and the Lord said unto Gideon, "Every one that lappeth of the water with his tongue, as a dog lappeth, him shalt thou set by himself; likewise every one that boweth down upon his knees to drink." And the number of them that lapped, putting their hand to their mouth, were three hundred men; but all the rest of the people bowed down upon their knees to drink water.

And the Lord said unto Gideon, "By the three hundred men that lapped will I save you."

And it came to pass the same night that the Lord said

unto him, "Arise, get thee down unto the host; for I have delivered it into thine hand."

And Gideon divided the three hundred men into three companies, and he put a trumpet in every man's hand, with empty pitchers, and lamps within the pitchers.

And he said unto them, "Look on me and do likewise; and, behold, when I come to the outside of the camp it shall be that, as I do, so shall ye do."

So Gideon, and the hundred men that were with him, came unto the outside of the camp in the beginning of the middle watch; and they had but newly set the watch; and they blew the trumpets and brake the pitchers that were in their hands. And the three companies blew the trumpets and brake the pitchers, and held the lamps in their left hands and the trumpets in their right hands to blow withal. And they cried, "The sword of the Lord, and of Gideon!" And the host fled.

JEPHTHAH'S DAUGHTER DANCES TO MEET HIM

Jephthah the Gileadite was a mighty man of valour. And Jephthah vowed a vow unto the Lord and said, "If thou shalt without fail deliver the children of Ammon into mine hands, then it shall be that whatsoever cometh forth of the doors of my house to meet me, when I return in peace from the children of Ammon, shall surely be the Lord's, and I will offer it up for a burnt offering."

So Jephthah passed over unto the children of Ammon to fight against them, and the Lord delivered them into his hands. And he smote them from Aroer, even till thou come to Minnith, even twenty cities, and unto the plain of the vineyards, with a very great slaughter.

And Jephthah came to Mizpeh unto his house, and, behold, his daughter came out to meet him with timbrels and with dances; and she was his only child.

And it came to pass, when he saw her, that he rent his clothes and said, "Alas, my daughter, thou hast brought me very low, and thou are one of them that trouble me, for I have opened my mouth unto the Lord, and I cannot go back."

And she said unto him, "My father, if thou has opened thy mouth unto the Lord, do to me according to that which hath proceeded out of thy mouth, forasmuch as the Lord hath taken vengeance for thee of thine enemies."

And she said unto her father, "Let this thing be done for me; let me alone two months, that I may go up and down upon the mountains, and bewail my virginity."

And he said, "Go!" And he sent her away.

And it came to pass at the end of two months that she returned unto her father, who did with her according to his vow which he had vowed.

There was a certain man of Zorah, of the family of the Danites, whose name was Manoah; and his wife was barren and bare not.

And the angel of the Lord appeared unto the woman and said unto her, "Behold now, thou art barren, but thou shalt conceive and bear a son. Now therefore beware, I pray thee, and drink not wine nor strong drink, and eat not any unclean thing. For, lo, thou shalt conceive and bear a son. And no razor shall come on his head, for the child shall be a Nazarite unto God from the womb; and he shall begin to deliver Israel out of the hand of the Philistines."

And the woman bare a son and called his name Samson; and the child grew, and the Lord blessed him.

And Samson went down to Timnath and saw a woman in Timnath of the daughters of the Philistines. And he came up and told his father and his mother and said, "I have seen a woman in Timnath of the daughters of the Philistines; now therefore get her for me to wife."

Then his father and his mother said unto him, "Is there never a woman among the daughters of thy brethren, or among all my people, that thou goest to take a wife of the uncircumcised Philistines?"

And Samson said unto his father, "Get her for me, for she pleaseth me well."

Then went Samson down, and his father and his mother, to Timnath, and came to the vineyards of Timnath; and, behold, a young lion roared against him. And the spirit of the Lord came mightily upon him, and he rent him as he would have rent a kid, and he had nothing in his hand; but he told not his father or his mother what he had done. And he went down and talked with the woman, and she pleased Samson well.

And after a time he returned to take her, and he turned aside to see the carcase of the lion, and, behold, there was a swarm of bees and honey in the carcase of the lion. And he took thereof in his hands and went on eating, and came to his father and mother, and he gave them, and they did eat, but he told not them that he had taken the honey out of the carcase of the lion.

So his father went down unto the woman, and Samson made there a feast, for so used the young men to do. And it came to pass, when they saw him, that they brought thirty companions to be with him.

And Samson said unto them, "I will now put forth a riddle unto you: if ye can certainly declare it me within the seven days of the feast, and find it out, then I will give you thirty sheets and thirty change of garments. But if ye cannot declare it me, then shall ye give me thirty sheets and thirty change of garments."

And they said unto him, "Put forth thy riddle, that we may hear it."

And he said unto them, "Out of the eater came forth meat, and out of the strong came forth sweetness." And they could not in three days expound the riddle.

And it came to pass on the seventh day that they said unto Samson's wife, "Entice thy husband, that he may declare unto us the riddle, lest we burn thee and thy father's house with fire."

And Samson's wife wept before him and said, "Thou lovest me not; thou hast put forth a riddle and hast not told it me."

And it came to pass on the seventh day that he told her,

because she lay sore upon him; and she told the riddle to the children of her people.

And the men of the city said unto him on the seventh day before the sun went down, "What is sweeter than honey? And what is stronger than a lion?"

And he said unto them, "If ye had not plowed with my heifer ye had not found out my riddle."

And the spirit of the Lord came upon him, and he went down to Ashkelon and slew thirty men of them and took their spoil, and gave change of garments unto them which expounded the riddle. And his anger was kindled, and he went up to his father's house.

Then the Philistines went up and pitched in Judah and spread themselves in Lehi.

And the men of Judah said, "Why are ye come up against us?"

And they answered, "To bind Samson are we come up, to do to him as he hath done to us."

Then three thousand men of Judah went to the top of the rock Etam and said to Samson, "Knowest thou not that the Philistines are rulers over us? What is this that thou hast done unto us?"

And he said unto them, "As they did unto me, so have I done unto them."

And they said unto him, "We are come down to bind thee, that we may deliver thee into the hand of the Philistines."

And Samson said unto them, "Swear unto me that ye will not fall upon me yourselves."

And they spake unto him, saying, "No, but we will bind thee fast and deliver thee into their hand; but surely we will not kill thee."

And they bound him with two new cords and brought

him up from the rock. And when he came unto Lehi the Philistines shouted against him; and the spirit of the Lord came mightily upon him, and the cords that were upon his arms became as flax that was burnt with fire, and his bands loosed from off his hands. And he found a new jawbone of an ass and put forth his hand and took it, and slew a thousand men therewith.

And it came to pass afterward that he loved a woman in the valley of Sorek whose name was Delilah.

And the lords of the Philistines came up unto her and said unto her, "Entice him, and see wherein his great strength lieth and by what means we may prevail against him, that we may bind him to afflict him; and we will give thee every one of us eleven hundred pieces of silver."

And Delilah said to Samson, "Tell me, I pray thee, wherein thy great strength lieth and wherewith thou mightest be bound to afflict thee."

And Samson said unto her, "If they bind me with seven green withs that were never dried, then shall I be weak and be as another man."

Then the lords of the Philistines brought up to her seven green withs which had not been dried, and she bound him with them. Now there were men lying in wait, abiding with her in the chamber.

And she said unto him, "The Philistines be upon thee, Samson." And he brake the withs as a thread of tow is broken when it toucheth the fire. So his strength was not known.

And Delilah said unto Samson, "Behold, thou hast mocked me and told me lies; now tell me, I pray thee, where with thou mightest be bound."

And he said unto her, "If they bind me fast with new ropes that never were occupied, then shall I be weak and be as another man."

Delilah therefore took new ropes and bound him therewith and said unto him, "The Philistines be upon thee, Samson." And there were liers in wait abiding in the chamber. And he brake them from off his arms like a thread.

And Delilah said unto Samson, "Hitherto thou hast mocked me and told me lies; tell me wherewith thou mightest be bound."

And he said unto her, "If thou weavest the seven locks of my head with a web."

And she fastened it with the pin and said unto him, "The Philistines be upon thee, Samson." And he awaked out of his sleep and went away with the pin of the beam and with the web.

And she said unto him, "How canst thou say, 'I love thee,' when thine heart is not with me? Thou hast mocked me these three times and hast not told me wherein thy great strength lieth."

And it came to pass, when she pressed him daily with her words and urged him, so that his soul was vexed unto death, that he told her all his heart and said unto her:

"There hath not come a razor upon mine head, for I have been a Nazarite unto God from my mother's womb. If I be shaven, then my strength will go from me and I shall become weak and be like any other man."

And when Delilah saw that he had told her all his heart she sent and called for the lords of the Philistines, saying, "Come up this once, for he hath shewed me all his heart."

Then the lords of the Philistines came up unto her and brought money in their hand. And she made him sleep upon her knees, and she called for a man, and she caused him to shave off the seven locks of his head; and she began to afflict him, and his strength went from him.

And she said, "The Philistines be upon thee, Samson!"

And he awoke out of his sleep and said, "I will go out as at other times before and shake myself." And he wist not that the Lord was departed from him.

But the Philistines took him and put out his eyes, and brought him down to Gaza and bound him with fetters of brass; and he did grind in the prison house. Howbeit the hair of his head began to grow again after he was shaven.

Then the lords of the Philistines gathered them together for to offer a great sacrifice unto Dagon, their god, and to rejoice, for they said, "Our god hath delivered Samson, our enemy, into our hand."

And when the people saw him they praised their god, for they said, "Our god hath delivered into our hands our enemy and the destroyer of our country, which slew many of us."

And it came to pass, when their hearts were merry, that they said, "Call for Samson, that he may make us sport."

And they called for Samson out of the prison house and he made them sport. And they set him between the pillars.

And Samson said unto the lad that held him by the hand, "Suffer me that I may feel the pillars whereupon the house standeth, that I may lean upon them."

Now the house was full of men and women, and all the lords of the Philistines were there, and there were upon the roof about three thousand men and women that beheld while Samson made sport.

And Samson called unto the Lord and said, "O Lord God, remember me, I pray thee, and strengthen me, I pray thee, only this once, O God, that I may be at once avenged of the Philistines for my two eyes."

And Samson took hold of the two middle pillars upon which the house stood and on which it was borne up, of the one with his right hand, and of the other with his left.

And Samson said, "Let me die with the Philistines." And he bowed himself with all his might, and the house fell upon the lords and upon all the people that were therein.

So the dead which he slew at his death were more than they which he slew in his life.

DAVID AND SOLOMON

The child Samuel ministered unto the Lord before Eli. And the word of the Lord was precious in those days; there was no open vision.

And it came to pass at that time, when Eli was laid down in his place and his eyes began to wax dim, that he could not see, and ere the lamp of God went out in the temple of the Lord, where the ark of God was, and Samuel was laid down to sleep, that the Lord called Samuel and he answered, "Here am I."

And he ran unto Eli and said, "Here am I, for thou calledst me."

And Eli said, "I called not. Lie down again." And he went and lay down.

And the Lord called yet again, "Samuel."

And Samuel arose and went to Eli and said, "Here am I, for thou didst call me."

And Eli answered, "I called not, my son. Lie down again."

Now Samuel did not yet know the Lord. And the Lord called Samuel again the third time. And he arose and went to Eli and said, "Here am I, for thou didst call me."

And Eli perceived that the Lord had called the child. Therefore Eli said unto Samuel, "Go, lie down, and it shall be, if he call thee, that thou shalt say, 'Speak, Lord, for thy servant heareth.'"

So Samuel went and lay down in his place. And the Lord came and stood and called as at other times, "Samuel, Samuel."

Then Samuel answered, "Speak, for thy servant heareth."

And the Lord said to Samuel, "Behold, I will do a thing in Israel at which both the ears of every one that heareth it shall tingle."

And Samuel lay until the morning, and opened the doors of the house of the Lord. And Samuel feared to shew Eli the vision.

Then Eli called Samuel and said, "Samuel, my son."

And he answered, "Here am I."

And Eli said, "What is the thing that the Lord hath said unto thee? I pray thee hide it not from me. God do so to thee, and more also, if thou hide any thing from me of all the things that he said unto thee."

And Samuel told him every whit and hid nothing from him.

And Eli said, "It is the Lord; let him do what seemeth him good."

And Samuel grew, and the Lord was with him and did let none of his words fall to the ground. And all Israel from Dan even to Beersheba knew that Samuel was established to be a prophet of the Lord.

And Samuel judged Israel all the days of his life.

And it came to pass, when Samuel was old, that he made his sons judges over Israel. And his sons walked not in his ways but turned aside after lucre, and took bribes and perverted judgment.

Then all the elders of Israel gathered themselves together and came to Samuel unto Ramah and said unto him, "Behold, thou art old, and thy sons walk not in thy ways. Now make us a king to judge us like all the nations."

But the thing displeased Samuel, when they said, "Give us a king to judge us." And Samuel prayed unto the Lord.

Nevertheless the people refused to obey the voice of Samuel, and they said, "Nay, but we will have a king over us."

And the Lord said to Samuel, "Hearken unto their voice and make them a king."

And Samuel said unto the men of Israel, "Go ye every man unto his city."

Now there was a man of Benjamin whose name was Kish, a Benjamite, a mighty man of power. And he had a son whose name was Saul, a choice young man and a goodly, and there was not among the children of Israel a goodlier person than he: from his shoulders and upward he was higher than any of the people.

And Samuel called the people together unto the Lord to Mizpeh and said unto the children of Israel, "Thus saith the Lord God of Israel. Now therefore present yourselves before the Lord by your tribes, and by your thousands."

And when Samuel had caused all the tribes of Israel to come near, the tribe of Benjamin was taken. When he had caused the tribe of Benjamin to come near by their families, the family of Matri was taken, and Saul, the son of Kish, was taken.

And Samuel said to all the people, "See ye him whom the Lord hath chosen, that there is none like him among all the people?"

And all the people shouted and said, "God save the king."

Now the Philistines gathered together their armies to battle and were gathered together at Shochoh, which belongeth to Judah, and pitched between Shochoh and Azekah, in Ephesdammim. And Saul and the men of Israel were gathered together and pitched by the valley of Elah, and set the battle in array against the Philistines.

And the Philistines stood on a mountain on the one side, and Israel stood on a mountain on the other side, and there was a valley between them. And there went out a champion out of the camp of the Philistines, named Goliath, of Gath, whose height was six cubits and a span.

And he had an helmet of brass upon his head and he was armed with a coat of mail; and the weight of the coat was five thousand shekels of brass. And he had greaves of brass upon his legs, and a target of brass between his shoulders. And the staff of his spear was like a weaver's beam, and his spear's head weighed six hundred shekels of iron; and one bearing a shield went before him.

And he stood and cried unto the armies of Israel and said unto them, "Why are ye come out to set your battle in array? Am not I a Philistine, and ye servants to Saul? Choose you a man for you and let him come down to me. If he be able to fight with me and to kill me, then will we be your servants; but if I prevail against him and kill him, then shall ye be our servants and serve us."

Now David was the son of that Ephrathite of Bethlehem-judah whose name was Jesse; and he had eight sons. And the man went among men for an old man in the days of Saul. And the three eldest sons of Jesse went and followed Saul to the battle. And David was the youngest.

And Jesse said unto David his son, "Take now for thy brethren an ephah of this parched corn, and these ten loaves, and run to the camp to thy brethren. And carry these ten cheeses unto the captain of their thousand and look how thy brethren fare and take their pledge."

And David rose up early in the morning and left the sheep with a keeper, and took and went, as Jesse had commanded him; and he came to the trench as the host was going forth to the fight and shouted for the battle. And as he talked with them, behold, there came up Goliath and spake according to the same words, and David heard them. And all the men of Israel, when they saw the man, fled from

him and were sore afraid.

And David spake to the men that stood by him, saying, "What shall be done to the man that killeth this Philistine and taketh away the reproach from Israel? For who is this Philistine that he should defy the armies of the living God?"

And Eliab, his eldest brother, heard when he spake unto the men; and Eliab's anger was kindled against David and he said, "Why camest thou down hither? And with whom hast thou left those few sheep in the wilderness? I know thy pride and the naughtiness of thine heart, for thou art come down that thou mightest see the battle."

And David said, "What have I now done? Is there not a cause?"

And when the words were heard which David spake, they rehearsed them before Saul and he sent for him.

And David said to Saul, "Let no man's heart fail because of him; thy servant will go and fight with this Philistine."

And Saul said to David, "Thou art not able to go against this Philistine to fight with him, for thou art but a youth, and he a man of war from his youth."

And David said unto Saul, "Thy servant kept his father's sheep, and there came a lion and a bear and took a lamb out of the flock. And I went out after him and smote him and delivered it out of his mouth, and when he arose against me I caught him by his beard and smote him and slew him.

"Thy servant slew both the lion and the bear; and this uncircumcised Philistine shall be as one of them, seeing he hath defied the armies of the living God."

David said moreover, "The Lord that delivered me out of the paw of the lion, and out of the paw of the bear, he will deliver me out of the hand of this Philistine."

And Saul said unto David, "Go, and the Lord be with thee." And Saul armed David with his armour, and he put an helmet of brass upon his head; also he armed him with a coat of mail. And David girded his sword upon his armour and he assayed to go, for he had not proved it.

And David said unto Saul, "I cannot go with these, for I have not proved them." And David put them off him. And he took his staff in his hand and chose him five smooth stones out of the brook and put them in a shepherd's bag which he had, even in a scrip; and his sling was in his hand; and he drew near to the Philistine.

And the Philistine came on and drew near unto David; and the man that bare the shield went before him. And when the Philistine looked about and saw David, he disdained him, for he was but a youth, and ruddy, and of a fair countenance.

And the Philistine said unto David, "Am I a dog, that thou comest to me with staves?" And the Philistine cursed David by his gods. And the Philistine said to David, "Come to me, and I will give thy flesh unto the fowls of the air and to the beasts of the field."

Then said David to the Philistine, "Thou comest to me with a sword and with a spear and with a shield; but I come to thee in the name of the Lord of hosts, the God of the armies of Israel, whom thou hast defied."

And David put his hand in his bag and took thence a stone, and slang it, and smote the Philistine in his forehead, that the stone sunk into his forehead; and he fell upon his face to the earth. So David prevailed over the Philistine with a sling and with a stone, and smote the Philistine and slew him; but there was no sword in the hand of David.

Therefore David ran and stood upon the Philistine, and took his sword and drew it out of the sheath thereof, and slew him and cut off his head therewith. And when the Philistines saw their champion was dead they fled.

DAVID CHALLENGES GOLIATH

The Lord is my shepherd:
  I shall not want.
He maketh me to lie down in green pastures;
  He leadeth me beside the still waters;
  He restoreth my soul.

He leadeth me in the paths of righteousness
  For his name's sake.
Yea, though I walk through the valley of the shadow of death,
  I will fear no evil,
  For thou art with me.

Psalm 23

PSALMS

Thy rod and thy staff,
  They comfort me.

Thou preparest a table before me
  In the presence of mine enemies;
Thou anointest my head with oil;
  My cup runneth over.
Surely goodness and mercy shall follow me
  All the days of my life,
And I will dwell in the house of the Lord
  Forever.

But the spirit of the Lord departed from Saul, and an evil spirit from the Lord troubled him.

And Saul's servants said unto him, "Behold now, an evil spirit from God troubleth thee. Let our Lord now command thy servants, which are before thee, to seek out a man who is a cunning player on an harp; and it shall come to pass, when the evil spirit from God is upon thee, that he shall play with his hand and thou shalt be well."

And Saul said unto his servants, "Provide me now a man that can play well and bring him to me."

Then answered one of the servants and said, "Behold, I have seen a son of Jesse the Bethlehemite that is cunning in playing, and a mighty valiant man, and a man of war, and prudent in matters, and a comely person, and the Lord is with him."

Wherefore Saul sent messengers unto Jesse and said, "Send me David, thy son, which is with the sheep."

And Jesse took an ass laden with bread, and a bottle of wine and a kid, and sent them by David, his son, unto Saul. And David came to Saul and stood before him, and he loved him greatly and he became his armour-bearer.

And Saul sent to Jesse, saying, "Let David, I pray thee, stand before me, for he hath found favour in my sight."

And it came to pass, when the evil spirit from God was upon Saul, that David took an harp and played with his hand: so Saul was refreshed and was well, and the evil spirit departed from him.

DAVID PLAYS AND SINGS FOR SAUL

And it came to pass that the soul of Jonathan, the son of Saul, was knit with the soul of David, and Jonathan loved him as his own soul. And Jonathan stripped himself of the robe that was upon him and gave it to David, and his garments, even to his sword, and to his bow and to his girdle.

And David went out whithersoever Saul sent him, and behaved himself wisely; and Saul set him over the men of war, and he was accepted in the sight of all the people and also in the sight of Saul's servants.

And it came to pass as they came, when David was returned from the slaughter of the Philistine, that the women came out of all cities of Israel, singing and dancing, to meet King Saul, with tabrets, with joy, and with instruments of music.

And the women answered one another as they played and said, "Saul hath slain his thousands, and David his ten thousands."

And Saul was very wroth, and the saying displeased him; and he said, "They have ascribed unto David ten thousands, and to me they have ascribed but thousands; and what can he have more but the kingdom?"

And Saul eyed David from that day and forward. And it came to pass on the morrow that the evil spirit from God came upon Saul, and he prophesied in the midst of the house; and David played with his hand, as at other times; and there was a javelin in Saul's hand.

And Saul cast the javelin, for he said, "I will smite David even to the wall with it."

And David avoided out of his presence twice. And Saul was afraid of David, because the Lord was with him and was departed from Saul. Therefore Saul removed him from him and made him his captain over a thousand; and he went out and came in before the people. But all Israel and Judah loved David, because he went out and came in before them.

And Michal, Saul's daughter, loved David; and they told Saul, and the thing pleased him.

And Saul said, "I will give him her, that she may be a snare to him and that the hand of the Philistines may be against him."

Wherefore Saul said to David, "Thou shalt this day be my son-in-law."

And Saul spake to Jonathan, his son, and to all his servants, that they should kill David.

And Jonathan told David, saying, "Saul, my father, seeketh to kill thee; now therefore, I pray thee, take heed to thyself until the morning and abide in a secret place and hide thyself. And I will go out and stand beside my father in the field where thou art, and I will commune with my father of thee; and what I see, that I will tell thee."

And Jonathan spake good of David unto Saul, his father, and said unto him, "Wherefore then wilt thou sin against innocent blood, to slay David without a cause?"

And Saul hearkened unto the voice of Jonathan, and Saul sware, "As the Lord liveth, he shall not be slain."

And the evil spirit from the Lord was upon Saul, as he sat in his house with his javelin in his hand; and David played with his hand. And Saul sought to smite David even to the wall with the javelin, but he slipped away out of Saul's presence and he smote the javelin into the wall; and David fled and escaped that night.

Saul also sent messengers unto David's house, to watch him, and to slay him in the morning. And Michal, David's wife, told him, saying, "If thou save not thy life tonight, tomorrow thou shalt be slain."

So Michal let David down through a window; and he went and fled and escaped. And Michal took an image and

JONATHAN WARNS DAVID TO FLEE

laid it in the bed, and put a pillow of goats' hair for his bolster and covered it with a cloth. And when Saul sent messengers to take David she said, "He is sick."

And Saul sent the messengers again to see David, saying, "Bring him up to me in the bed, that I may slay him." And when the messengers were come in, behold, there was an image in the bed, with a pillow of goats' hair for his bolster.

And Saul said unto Michal, "Why hast thou deceived me so and sent away mine enemy, that he is escaped?"

And David fled from Naioth in Ramah and came and said before Jonathan, "What have I done? What is mine iniquity? And what is my sin before thy father, that he seeketh my life?"

And Jonathan said unto him, "God forbid. Thou shalt not die. Behold, my father will do nothing either great or small but that he will shew it me; and why should my father hide this thing from me? It is not so."

And David sware moreover and said, "Thy father certainly knoweth that I have found grace in thine eyes, and he saith, 'Let not Jonathan know this, lest he be grieved'; but truly as the Lord liveth, and as thy soul liveth, there is but a step between me and death."

And Jonathan caused David to swear again, because he loved him, for he loved him as he loved his own soul. Then Jonathan said to David:

"Tomorrow is the new moon, and thou shalt be missed because thy seat will be empty. Then thou shalt go down quickly and come to the place where thou didst hide thyself when the business was in hand, and shalt remain by the stone Ezel. And I will shoot three arrows on the side thereof, as though I shot at a mark. And, behold, I will send a lad, saying, 'Go, find out the arrows.' If I expressly say unto the lad, 'Behold, the arrows are on this side of thee, take them,' then come thou, for there is peace to thee, and no hurt, as the Lord liveth. But if I say thus unto the young man, 'Behold, the arrows are beyond thee,' go thy way, for the Lord hath sent thee away."

And it came to pass in the morning that Jonathan went out into the field at the time appointed with David, and a little lad with him.

And he said unto his lad, "Run, find out now the arrows which I shoot."

And as the lad ran he shot an arrow beyond him. And when the lad was come to the place of the arrow which Jonathan had shot, Jonathan cried after the lad and said, "Is not the arrow beyond thee?" And Jonathan cried after the lad, "Make speed, haste, stay not." And Jonathan's lad gathered up the arrows and came to his master. But the lad knew not any thing; only Jonathan and David knew the matter.

And Jonathan gave his artillery unto his lad and said unto him, "Go, carry them to the city."

And as soon as the lad was gone David arose out of a place toward the south and fell on his face to the ground and bowed himself three times; and they kissed one another and wept one with another, until David exceeded.

And Jonathan said to David, "Go in peace, forasmuch as we have sworn both of us in the name of the Lord, saying, 'The Lord be between me and thee, and between my seed and thy seed for ever.'"

And he arose and departed, and Jonathan went into the city.

Now Samuel was dead, and all Israel had lamented him. And Saul had put away those that had familiar spirits, and the wizards, out of the land.

And the Philistines gathered themselves together and came and pitched in Shunem, and Saul gathered all Israel together and they pitched in Gilboa. And when Saul saw the host of the Philistines he was afraid, and his heart greatly trembled. And when Saul inquired of the Lord, the Lord answered him not.

Then said Saul unto his servants, "Seek me a woman that hath a familiar spirit, that I may go to her and inquire of her."

And his servants said to him, "Behold, there is a woman that hath a familiar spirit at Endor."

And Saul disguised himself and put on other raiment, and he went, and two men with him, and they came to the woman by night, and he said, "I pray thee, divine unto me by the familiar spirit, and bring me him up whom I shall name unto thee."

And the woman said unto him, "Behold, thou knowest what Saul hath done, how he hath cut off those that have familiar spirits, and the wizards, out of the land: wherefore, then, layest thou a snare for my life, to cause me to die?"

And Saul sware to her by the Lord, saying, "As the Lord liveth, there shall no punishment happen to thee for this thing."

Then said the woman, "Whom shall I bring up?"

And he said, "Bring me up Samuel."

And when the woman saw Samuel she cried with a loud voice, and the woman spake to Saul, saying, "Why hast thou deceived me? For thou art Saul."

And the king said unto her, "Be not afraid. For what sawest thou?"

And the woman said unto Saul, "I saw gods ascending out of the earth."

And he said unto her, "What form is he of?"

And she said, "An old man cometh up, and he is covered with a mantle."

And Saul perceived that it was Samuel, and he stooped with his face to the ground and bowed himself.

And Samuel said to Saul, "Why hast thou disquieted me, to bring me up?"

And Saul answered, "I am sore distressed, for the Philistines make war against me, and God is departed from me and answereth me no more, neither by prophets nor by dreams. Therefore I have called thee, that thou mayest make known unto me what I shall do."

Then said Samuel, "Wherefore then dost thou ask of me, seeing the Lord is departed from thee and is become thine enemy? And the Lord hath done to him as he spake by me: for the Lord hath rent the kingdom out of thine hand and given it to thy neighbour, even to David."

Now the Philistines fought against Israel, and the men of Israel fled from before the Philistines and fell down slain in Mount Gilboa. And the Philistines followed hard upon Saul and upon his sons; and the Philistines slew Jonathan and Abinadab and Melchishua, Saul's sons. And the battle went sore against Saul, and the archers hit him; and he was sore wounded of the archers. Then said Saul unto his armour-bearer, "Draw thy sword and thrust me through therewith, lest these uncircumcised come and thrust me through, and abuse me." But his armour-bearer would not, for he was sore afraid. Therefore Saul took a sword and fell upon it.

And when his armour-bearer saw that Saul was dead, he fell likewise upon his sword and died with him. So Saul died, and his three sons, and his armour-bearer, and all his men, that same day together.

Now it came to pass, after the death of Saul, David lamented with this lamentation over Saul and over Jonathan, his son:

The beauty of Israel is slain upon thy high places: how are the mighty fallen! Tell it not in Gath, publish it not in the streets of Askelon, lest the daughters of the Philistines rejoice, lest the daughters of the uncircumcised triumph.

"Ye mountains of Gilboa, let there be no dew, neither let there be rain, upon you, nor fields of offerings, for there the shield of the mighty is vilely cast away, the shield of Saul, as though he had not been anointed with oil.

"From the blood of the slain, from the fat of the mighty, the bow of Jonathan turned not back, and the sword of Saul returned not empty. Saul and Jonathan were lovely and pleasant in their lives, and in their death they were not divided: they were swifter than eagles; they were stronger than lions.

"Ye daughters of Israel, weep over Saul, who clothed you in scarlet, with other delights, who put on ornaments of gold upon your apparel.

"How are the mighty fallen in the midst of the battle! O Jonathan, thou wast slain in thine high places. I am distressed for thee, my brother Jonathan. Very pleasant hast thou been unto me; thy love to me was wonderful, passing the love of women. How are the mighty fallen, and the weapons of war perished!"

And the men of Judah came, and there they anointed David king over the house of Judah. Now there was long war between the house of Saul and the house of David, but David waxed stronger and stronger, and the house of Saul waxed weaker and weaker.

And unto David were sons born in Hebron, and his firstborn was Amnon, of Ahinoam the Jezreelitess. And his second, Chileab, of Abigail, the wife of Nabal the Carmelite; and the third, Absalom, the son of Maacah, the daughter of Talmai, king of Geshur.

David was thirty years old when he began to reign, and he reigned forty years. In Hebron he reigned over Judah seven years and six months, and in Jerusalem he reigned thirty and three years over all Israel and Judah. And the king and his men went to Jerusalem. So David dwelt in the fort and called it the city of David. And David built round about from Millo and inward.

And David took him more concubines and wives out of Jerusalem, after he was come from Hebron, and there were yet sons and daughters born to David. And these be the names of those that were born unto him in Jerusalem: Shammuah and Shobab and Nathan and Solomon.

And the Philistines came up yet again and spread themselves in the valley of Rephaim. And when David enquired of the Lord he said, "Thou shalt not go up, but fetch a compass behind them and come upon them over against the mulberry trees. And let it be, when thou hearest the sound of a going in the tops of the mulberry trees, that then thou shalt bestir thyself, for then shall the Lord go out before thee to smite the host of the Philistines."

And David did so, as the Lord had commanded him, and smote the Philistines from Geba until thou come to Gazer.

And Absalom spake unto his brother Amnon neither good or bad, for Absalom hated Amnon.

And it came to pass that tidings came to David, saying, "Absalom hath slain all the king's sons, and there is not one of them left." Then the king arose and tare his garments and lay on the earth, and all his servants stood by with their clothes rent.

And Jonadab, the son of Shimeah, David's brother, answered and said, "Let not my lord suppose that they have slain all the young men, the king's sons, for Amnon only is dead."

So Absalom fled and went to Geshur, and was there three years. And the soul of King David longed to go forth unto Absalom.

And the king said unto Joab, "Go therefore, bring the young man Absalom again."

So Joab arose and went to Geshur and brought Absalom to Jerusalem.

And the king said, "Let him turn to his own house, and let him not see my face."

So Absalom returned to his own house and saw not the king's face. But in all Israel there was none to be so much praised as Absalom for his beauty; from the sole of his foot even to the crown of his head there was no blemish in him. And when he polled his head (for it was at every year's end that he polled it, because the hair was heavy on him, therefore he polled it) he weighed the hair of his head at two hundred skekels after the king's weight.

And Absalom dwelt two full years in Jerusalem and saw not the king's face. And it came to pass after this that Absalom prepared him chariots and horses, and fifty men to run before him. And Absalom rose up early and stood beside the way of the gate, and it was so that when any man that had a controversy came to the king for judgment, then Absalom called unto him and said, "Of what city art thou?"

And he said, "Thy servant is of one of the tribes of Israel."

And Absalom said unto him, "See, thy matters are good and right, but there is no man deputed of the king to hear thee." Absalom said moreover, "Oh, that I were made judge in the land, that every man which hath any suit or cause might come unto me and I would do him justice!"

And it was so that when any man came nigh to him to do him obeisance, he put forth his hand and took him and kissed him. And on this manner did Absalom to all Israel that came to the king for judgment; so Absalom stole the hearts of the men of Israel.

And there came a messenger to David, saying, "The hearts of the men of Israel are after Absalom."

And David said unto all his servants that were with him at Jerusalem, "Arise and let us flee, for we shall not else escape from Absalom."

Then David came to Mahanaim, and Absalom passed over Jordan, he and all the men of Israel with him. And David numbered the people that were with him, and set captains of thousands and captains of hundreds over them. And David sent forth a third part of the people under the hand of Joab, and a third part under the hand of Abishai, the son of Zeruiah, Joab's brother, and a third part under the hand of Ittai the Gittite.

And the king commanded Joab and Abishai and Ittai, saying, "Deal gently for my sake with the young man, even with Absalom."

So the people went out into the field against Israel, and the battle was in the wood of Ephraim, where the people of Israel were slain before the servants of David. And there was there a great slaughter that day of twenty thousand men, for the battle was there scattered over the face of all the country, and the wood devoured more people that day than the sword devoured.

And Absalom met the servants of David. And Absalom rode upon a mule, and the mule went under the thick boughs of a great oak, and his head caught hold of the oak, and he was taken up between the heaven and the earth, and the mule that was under him went away.

And a certain man saw it and told Joab and said, "Behold, I saw Absalom hanged in an oak."

And Joab said unto the man that told him, "And, behold, thou sawest him, and why didst thou not smite him there to the ground? And I would have given thee ten shekels of silver and a girdle."

And the man said unto Joab, "Though I should receive a thousand shekels of silver in mine hand, yet would I not put forth mine hand against the king's son, for in our hearing the king charged thee and Abishai and Ittai, saying, 'Beware that none touch the young man Absalom.' Otherwise I should have wrought falsehood against mine own life, for there is no matter hid from the king, and thou thyself wouldest have set thyself against me."

Then said Joab, "I may not tarry thus with thee." And he took three darts in his hand and thrust them through the heart of Absalom, while he was yet alive in the midst of the oak. And ten young men that bare Joab's armour compassed about and smote Absalom and slew him.

And Joab blew the trumpet, and the people returned from pursuing after Israel, for Joab held back the people. And they took Absalom and cast him into a great pit in the wood and laid a very great heap of stones upon him, and all Israel fled every one to his tent.

And David sat between the two gates, and the watchman went up to the roof over the gate unto the wall, and lifted up his eyes and looked, and behold a man running alone. And the watchman cried and told the king.

And the king said, "If he be alone there is tidings in his mouth," and he came apace and drew near.

And the watchman saw another man running, and the watchman called unto the porter and said, "Behold, another man running alone."

And the king said, "He also bringeth tidings."

And the watchman said, "Me thinketh the running of the foremost is like the running of Ahimaaz, the son of Zadok."

And the king said, "He is a good man and cometh with good tidings."

And Ahimaaz called and said unto the king, "All is well." And he fell down to the earth upon his face before the king and said, "Blessed be the Lord, thy God, which hath delivered up the men that lifted up their hand against my lord the king."

And the king said, "Is the young man Absalom safe?"

And Ahimaaz answered, "When Joab sent the king's servant and me, thy servant, I saw a great tumult but I knew not what it was."

And the king said unto him, "Turn aside, and stand here." And he turned aside and stood still.

And, behold, Cushi came, and Cushi said, "Tidings, my lord the king, for the Lord hath avenged thee this day of all them that rose up against thee."

And the king said unto Cushi, "Is the young man Absalom safe?"

And Cushi answered, "The enemies of my lord the king, and all that rise against thee to do thee hurt, be as that young man is."

And the king was much moved and went up to the chamber over the gate, and wept, and as he went, thus he said: "O my son Absalom, my son, my son Absalom! Would God I had died for thee, O Absalom, my son, my son!"

David and
Absalom
II SAMUEL

N ow the days of David drew nigh that he should die, and he charged Solomon, his son, saying, "I go the way of all the earth. Be thou strong therefore and shew thyself a man. And keep the charge of the Lord, thy God, to walk in his ways, to keep his statutes and his commandments."

So David slept with his fathers and was buried in the city of David. Then sat Solomon upon the throne of David, his father, and his kingdom was established greatly.

In Gibeon the Lord appeared to Solomon in a dream by night, and God said, "Ask what I shall give thee."

And Solomon said, "O Lord, my God, thou hast made thy servant king instead of David, my father, and I am but a little child: I know not how to go out or come in. Give therefore thy servant an understanding heart to judge thy people, that I may discern between good and bad, for who is able to judge this thy so great a people?"

And the speech pleased the Lord, that Solomon had asked this thing.

Then came there two women unto the king and stood before him.

And the one woman said, "O my lord, I and this woman dwell in one house, and I was delivered of a child with her in the house. And it came to pass the third day after that I was delivered that this woman was delivered also, and we were together; there was no stranger with us in the house, save we two in the house. And this woman's child died in the night because she overlaid it. And she arose at midnight and took my son from beside me, while thine handmaid slept, and laid it in her bosom and laid her dead child in my bosom. And when I rose in the morning to give my child suck, behold, it was dead, but when I had considered it in the morning, behold, it was not my son which I did bear."

And the other woman said, "Nay, but the living is my son and the dead is thy son."

And this said, "No, but the dead is thy son and the living is my son." Thus they spake before the king.

And the king said, "Bring me a sword." And they brought a sword before the king. And the king said, "Divide the living child in two and give half to the one and half to the other."

Then spake the woman whose the living child was unto the king, for her bowels yearned upon her son, and she said, "O my lord, give her the living child and in no wise slay it."

But the other said, "Let it be neither mine nor thine, but divide it."

Then the king answered and said, "Give her the living child and in no wise slay it; she is the mother thereof."

And all Israel heard of the judgment which the king had judged; and they feared the king, for they saw that the wisdom of God was in him, to do judgment.

"GIVE HER THE LIVING CHILD"

And Hiram, king of Tyre, sent his servants unto Solomon, for he had heard that they had anointed him king in the room of his father, for Hiram was ever a lover of David.

And Solomon sent to Hiram, saying, "Thou knowest how that David, my father, could not build an house unto the name of the Lord, his God, for the wars which were about him on every side, until the Lord put them under the soles of his feet. But now the Lord, my God, hath given me rest on every side, so that there is neither adversary nor evil occurrent. And, behold, I purpose to build an house unto the name of the Lord, my God, as the Lord spake unto David, my father, saying, 'Thy son, whom I will set upon thy throne in thy room, he shall build an house unto my name.'

"Now therefore command thou that they hew me cedar trees out of Lebanon. And my servants shall be with thy servants, and unto thee will I give hire for thy servants according to all that thou shalt appoint, for thou knowest that there is not among us any that can skill to hew timber like unto the Sidonians."

And it came to pass, when Hiram heard the words of Solomon, that he rejoiced greatly and said, "Blessed be the Lord this day, which hath given unto David a wise son over this great people."

And it came to pass in the four hundred and eightieth year after the children of Israel were come out of the land of Egypt, in the fourth year of Solomon's reign over Israel, that he began to build the house of the Lord. So he built the house and finished it, and covered the house with beams and boards of cedar.

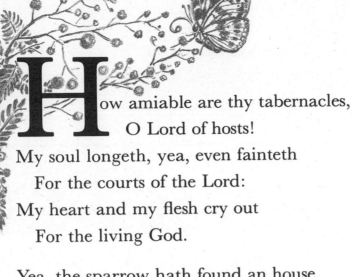

How amiable are thy tabernacles,
     O Lord of hosts!
My soul longeth, yea, even fainteth
     For the courts of the Lord:
My heart and my flesh cry out
     For the living God.

Yea, the sparrow hath found an house,
     And the swallow a nest for herself,
     Where she may lay her young.
     Even thine altars! O Lord of hosts,
     My king and my God!

Blessed are they that dwell in thy house:
     They will be still praising thee.

Blessed is the man whose strength is in thee,
     In whose heart are the ways of them.

Who passing through the valley of weeping make it a well;
     The rain also filleth the pools.

Behold, O God our shield,
     And look upon the face of thine anointed!

For a day in thy courts is better
     Than a thousand.
I had rather be a doorkeeper in the house of my God
     Than to dwell in the tents of wickedness.

Psalm 84

PSALMS
155

CUTTING THE CEDARS OF LEBANON FOR SOLOMON'S TEMPLE

For the Lord God is a sun and shield:
   The Lord will give grace and glory;
No good thing will he withhold
   From them that walk uprightly.

O Lord of hosts, blessed is the man
   That trusteth in thee!

Lift up your heads, O ye gates;
   And be ye lift up, ye everlasting doors!
   And the king of glory shall come in.
Who is this king of glory?
   The Lord, strong and mighty!
   The Lord, mighty in battle!

Lift up your heads, O ye gates;
   Even lift them up, ye everlasting doors!
   And the king of glory shall come in.
Who is this king of glory?
   The Lord of hosts!
   He is the king of glory!

And when the queen of Sheba heard of the fame of Solomon concerning the name of the Lord, she came to prove him with hard questions. And she came to Jerusalem with a very great train, with camels that bare spices, and very much gold, and precious stones; and when she was come to Solomon she communed with him of all that was in her heart.

And Solomon told her all her questions; there was not any thing hid from the king which he told her not. And when the queen of Sheba had seen all Solomon's wisdom, and the house that he had built, and the meat of his table, and the sitting of his servants, and the attendance of his ministers, and their apparel, and his cupbearers, and his ascent by which he went up unto the house of the Lord, there was no more spirit in her.

And she said to the king, "It was a true report that I heard in mine own land of thy acts and of thy wisdom. Howbeit I believed not the words, until I came and mine eyes had seen it. And, behold, the half was not told me: thy wisdom and prosperity exceedeth the fame which I heard."

And she gave the king an hundred and twenty talents of gold, and of spices very great store, and precious stones; there came no more such abundance of spices as these which the queen of Sheba gave to King Solomon.

And the navy also of Hiram, that brought gold from Ophir, brought in from Ophir great plenty of almug trees and precious stones. And the king made of the almug trees pillars for the house of the Lord, and for the king's house, harps also and psalteries for singers; there came no such almug trees, nor were seen unto this day.

And King Solomon gave unto the queen of Sheba all her desire, whatsoever she asked, beside that which Solomon gave her of his royal bounty. So she turned and went to her own country, she and her servants.

And the time that Solomon reigned in Jerusalem over all Israel was forty years. And Solomon slept with his fathers and was buried in the city of David, his father; and Rehoboam, his son, reigned in his stead.

THE PROPHETS

In the thirty and eighth year of Asa, king of Judah, began Ahab, the son of Omri, to reign over Israel; and Ahab, the son of Omri, reigned over Israel in Samaria twenty and two years. And Ahab, the son of Omri, did evil in the sight of the Lord above all that were before him. And he reared up an altar for Baal in the house of Baal which he had built in Samaria. And Ahab made a grove.

And Elijah the Tishbite, who was of the inhabitants of Gilead, said unto Ahab, "As the Lord God of Israel liveth, before whom I stand, there shall not be dew nor rain these years but according to my word."

And the word of the Lord came unto Elijah, saying, "Get thee hence, and turn thee eastward and hide thyself by the brook Cherith that is before Jordan. And it shall be that thou shalt drink of the brook; and I have commanded the ravens to feed thee there." So he went and did according unto the word of the Lord. And it came to pass that after a while the brook dried up, because there had been no rain in the land.

Elijah's
Miracles
I KINGS
160

And the word of the Lord came unto him, saying, "Arise, get thee to Zarephath, which belongeth to Zidon, and dwell there; behold, I have commanded a widow woman there to sustain thee."

So he arose and went to Zarephath. And when he came to the gate of the city, behold, the widow woman was there gathering of sticks; and he called to her and said, "Fetch me, I pray thee, a little water in a vessel, that I may drink." And as she was going to fetch it he called to her and said, "Bring me, I pray thee, a morsel of bread in thine hand."

And she said, "As the Lord, thy God, liveth, I have not a cake but an handful of meal in a barrel and a little oil in a cruse; and, behold, I am gathering two sticks, that I may go in and dress it for me and my son, that we may eat it and die."

And Elijah said unto her, "Fear not. Go and do as thou has said, but make me thereof a little cake first and bring it unto me, and after make for thee and for thy son. For thus saith the Lord God of Israel, 'The barrel of meal shall not waste, neither shall the cruse of oil fail, until the day that the Lord sendeth rain upon the earth.'" And she went and did according to the saying of Elijah; and she and he and her house did eat many days. And the barrel of meal wasted not, neither did the cruse of oil fail, according to the word of the Lord, which he spake by Elijah.

And it came to pass after these things that the son of the woman, the mistress of the house, fell sick; and his sickness was so sore that there was no breath left in him.

And she said unto Elijah, "What have I to do with thee, O thou man of God? Art thou come unto me to call my sin to remembrance and to slay my son?"

And he said unto her, "Give me thy son." And he took him out of her bosom and carried him up into a loft, where he abode, and laid him upon his own bed.

And he cried unto the Lord and said, "O Lord, my God, hast thou also brought evil upon the widow with whom I sojourn, by slaying her son?" And he stretched himself upon the child three times and cried unto the Lord and said, "O Lord, my God, I pray thee, let this child's soul come into him again."

And the Lord heard the voice of Elijah; and the soul of the child came into him again and he revived.

And Elijah took the child and brought him down out of the chamber into the house and delivered him unto his mother; and Elijah said, "See, thy son liveth."

And the woman said to Elijah, "Now by this I know that thou art a man of God and that the word of the Lord in thy mouth is truth."

Aad it came to pass, when Ahab saw Elijah, that Ahab said unto him, "Art thou he that troubleth Israel?"

And he answered, "I have not troubled Israel; but thou, and thy father's house, in that ye have forsaken the commandments of the Lord, and thou hast followed Baalim. Now therefore send and gather to me all Israel unto Mount Carmel, and the prophets of Baal four hundred and fifty, and the prophets of the groves four hundred, which eat at Jezebel's table."

So Ahab sent unto all the children of Israel and gathered the prophets together unto Mount Carmel.

And Elijah came unto all the people and said, "How long halt ye between two opinions? If the Lord be God, follow him; but if Baal, then follow him."

And the people answered him not a word.

Then said Elijah unto the people, "I, even I only, remain a prophet of the Lord; but Baal's prophets are four hundred and fifty men. Let them therefore give us two bullocks, and let them choose one bullock for themselves, and cut it in pieces and lay it on wood and put no fire under; and I will dress the other bullock and lay it on wood and put no fire under. And call ye on the name of your gods, and I will call on the name of the Lord; and the God that answereth by fire, let him be God.

And all the people answered and said, "It is well spoken."

And they took the bullock which was given them, and they dressed it and called on the name of Baal from morning even until noon, saying, "O Baal, hear us." But there was no voice, nor any that answered. And they leaped upon the altar which was made.

And it came to pass at noon that Elijah mocked them and said, "Cry aloud, for he is a god; either he is talking, or he is pursuing, or he is in a journey, or peradventure he sleepeth and must be awaked."

And they cried aloud, and cut themselves after their manner with knives and lancets, till the blood gushed out upon them. And it came to pass, when midday was past, and they prophesied until the time of the offering of the evening sacrifice, that there was neither voice nor any to answer nor any that regarded.

And Elijah said unto all the people, "Come near unto me."

And all the people came near unto him. And he repaired the altar of the Lord that was broken down. And Elijah took twelve stones, according to the number of the tribes of the sons of Jacob, unto whom the word of the Lord came, saying, "Israel shall be thy name." And with the stones he built an altar in the name of the Lord; and he made a trench about the altar, as great as would contain two measures of seed. And he put the wood in order, and cut the bullock in pieces and laid him on the wood, and said, "Fill four barrels with water and pour it on the burnt sacrifice and on the wood."

And he said, "Do it the second time." And they did it the second time.

And he said, "Do it the third time." And they did it the third time. And the water ran round about the altar; and he filled the trench also with water.

And it came to pass at the time of the offering of the evening sacrifice that Elijah, the prophet, came near and said, "Lord God of Abraham, Isaac, and of Israel, let it be known this day that thou art God in Israel and that I am thy servant and that I have done all these things at thy word. Hear me, O Lord, hear me, that this people may know that thou art the Lord God and that thou hast turned their heart back again." Then the fire of the Lord fell and consumed the burnt sacrifice, and the wood, and the stones, and the dust, and licked up the water that was in the trench

And when all the people saw it they fell on their faces and they said, "The Lord, he is the God; the Lord, he is the God!"

And Elijah said unto them, "Take the prophets of Baal. Let not one of them escape." And they took them. And Elijah brought them down to the brook Kishon and slew them there.

And Ahab told Jezebel all that Elijah had done, and withal how he had slain all the prophets with the sword. Then Jezebel sent a messenger unto Elijah, saying:

"So let the gods do to me, and more also, if I make not thy life as the life of one of them by tomorrow about this time."

And when he saw that he arose and went for his life unto Horeb, the mount of God. And he came thither unto a cave and lodged there; and, behold, the word of the Lord came to him, and he said unto him, "What doest thou here, Elijah?"

And he said, "I have been very jealous for the Lord God of hosts, for the children of Israel have forsaken thy covenant, thrown down thine altars, and slain thy prophets with the sword; and I, even I only, am left; and they seek my life, to take it away."

And he said, "Go forth and stand upon the mount before the Lord."

And, behold, the Lord passed by, and a great and strong wind rent the mountains and brake in pieces the rocks before the Lord, but the Lord was not in the wind. And after the wind an earthquake, but the Lord was not in the earthquake. And after the earthquake a fire, but the Lord was not in the fire. And after the fire a still small voice.

And it was so when Elijah heard it that he wrapped his face in his mantle and went out and stood in the entering in of the cave.

And the Lord said unto him, "Go, return on thy way to the wilderness of Damascus; and when thou comest, anoint Hazael to be king over Syria. And Jehu, the son of Nimshi, shalt thou anoint to be king over Israel; and Elisha, the son of Shaphat, shalt thou anoint to be prophet in thy room."

So Elijah departed thence and found Elisha, the son of Shaphat, who was plowing. And he left the oxen and ran after Elijah and said, "Let me, I pray thee, kiss my father and my mother, and then I will follow thee."

And it came to pass after these things that Naboth the Jezreelite had a vineyard which was in Jezreel, hard by the palace of Ahab, king of Samaria. And Ahab spake unto Naboth, saying, "Give me thy vineyard that I may have it for a garden of herbs, because it is near unto my house; and I will give thee for it a better vineyard than it, or, if it seem good to thee, I will give thee the worth of it in money."

And Naboth said to Ahab, "The Lord forbid it me that I should give the inheritance of my fathers unto thee."

And Ahab came into his house, heavy and displeased because of the word which Naboth the Jezreelite had spoken to him. And he laid him down upon his bed and turned away his face and would eat no bread.

But Jezebel, his wife, came to him and said unto him, "Why is thy spirit so sad, that thou eatest no bread?"

And he said unto her, "Because I spake unto Naboth

the Jezreelite and said unto him, 'Give me thy vineyard for money, or else, if it please thee, I will give thee another vineyard for it,' and he answered, 'I will not give thee my vineyard.'"

And Jezebel, his wife, said unto him, "Dost thou now govern the kingdom of Israel? Arise and eat bread and let thine heart be merry. I will give thee the vineyard of Naboth the Jezreelite."

So she wrote letters in Ahab's name and sealed them with his seal and sent the letters unto the elders and to the nobles that were in his city, dwelling with Naboth. And she wrote

in the letters, saying, "Proclaim a fast and set Naboth on high among the people; and set two men, sons of Belial, before him, to bear witness against him, saying, 'Thou didst blaspheme God and the king.' And then carry him out and stone him, that he may die."

And the men of his city, even the elders and the nobles who were the inhabitants in his city, did as Jezebel had sent unto them. Then they sent to Jezebel, saying, "Naboth is stoned and is dead."

And it came to pass, when Jezebel heard that Naboth was stoned and was dead, that Jezebel said to Ahab, "Arise, take possession of the vineyard of Naboth the Jezreelite, which he refused to give thee for money, for Naboth is not alive but dead."

And the word of the Lord came to Elijah the Tishbite, saying, "Arise, go down to meet Ahab, king of Israel, which is in Samaria; behold, he is in the vineyard of Naboth, whither he is gone down to possess it."

And Ahab said to Elijah, "Hast thou found me, O mine enemy?"

And he answered, "I have found thee, because thou hast sold thyself to work evil in the sight of the Lord. Behold, I will bring evil upon thee."

And of Jezebel also spake the Lord, saying, "The dogs shall eat Jezebel by the wall of Jezreel."

And it came to pass, when Ahab heard those words, that he rent his clothes and put sackcloth upon his flesh, and fasted, and lay in sackcloth, and went softly.

And the word of the Lord came to Elijah the Tishbite, saying, "Seest thou how Ahab humbleth himself before me. Because he humbleth himself before me I will not bring the evil in his days, but in his son's days will I bring the evil upon his house."

And it came to pass, when the Lord would take up Elijah into heaven by a whirlwind, that Elijah went with Elisha from Gilgal.

And it came to pass, as they still went on, and talked, that, behold, there appeared a chariot of fire, and horses of fire, and parted them both asunder; and Elijah went up by a whirlwind into heaven.

And Elisha saw it, and he cried, "My father, my father, the chariot of Israel and the horsemen thereof!" And he saw Elijah no more; and he took hold of his own clothes and rent them in two pieces. He took up also the mantle of Elijah that fell from him, and went back and stood by the bank of Jordan.

Now Naaman, captain of the host of the king of Syria, was a great man with his master, and honourable, because by him the Lord had given deliverance unto Syria; he was also a mighty man in valour, but he was a leper.

And the Syrians had gone out by companies and had brought away captive out of the land of Israel a little maid; and she waited on Naaman's wife.

And she said unto her mistress, "Would God my lord were with the prophet that is in Samaria, for he would recover him of his leprosy."

And one went in and told his lord, saying, "Thus and thus said the maid that is of the land of Israel."

And the king of Syria said, "Go to, go, and I will send a letter unto the king of Israel."

And Naaman departed and took with him ten talents of silver and six thousand pieces of gold and ten changes of raiment. And he brought the letter to the king of Israel, saying, "Now when this letter is come unto thee, behold, I have therewith sent Naaman, my servant, to thee that thou mayest recover him of his leprosy."

And it came to pass, when the king of Israel had read the letter, that he rent his clothes and said, "Am I God, to kill and to make alive, that this man doth send unto me to recover a man of his leprosy? Wherefore consider, I pray you, and see how he seeketh a quarrel against me."

And it was so, when Elisha, the man of God, had heard that the king of Israel had rent his clothes, that he sent to the king, saying, "Wherefore hast thou rent thy clothes? Let him come now to me and he shall know that there is a prophet in Israel."

So Naaman came with his horses and with his chariot and stood at the door of the house of Elisha.

And Elisha sent a messenger unto him, saying, "Go and

wash in Jordan seven times, and thy flesh shall come again to thee and thou shalt be clean."

But Naaman was wroth and went away, and said, "Behold, I thought, 'He will surely come out to me, and stand and call on the name of the Lord, his God, and strike his hand over the place and recover the leper.' Are not Abana and Pharpar, rivers of Damascus, better than all the waters of Israel? May I not wash in them and be clean?" So he turned and went away in a rage.

And his servants came near and spake unto him and said, "My father, if the prophet had bid thee do some great thing, wouldest thou not have done it? How much rather then, when he saith to thee, 'Wash, and be clean'?"

Then went he down and dipped himself seven times in Jordan, according to the saying of the man of God; and his flesh came again like unto the flesh of a little child and he was clean.

And Elisha, the prophet, called one of the children of the prophets and said unto him, "Gird up thy loins and take this box of oil in thine hand and go to Ramoth-gilead. And when thou comest thither, look out there Jehu, the son of Jehoshaphat, the son of Nimshi, and carry him to an inner chamber. Then take the box of oil and pour it on his head, and say, 'Thus saith the Lord: "I have anointed thee king over Israel.'' Then open the door and flee and tarry not."

So the young man, even the young man the prophet, went to Ramoth-gilead. And when he came, behold, the captains of the host were sitting.

And he said, "I have an errand to thee, O Captain."

And Jehu said, "Unto which of all us?"

And he said, "To thee, O Captain." And he went into the house; and he poured the oil on his head and said unto him, "Thus saith the Lord God of Israel: 'I have anointed thee king over the people of the Lord, even over Israel. And thou shalt smite the house of Ahab, thy master, that I may avenge the blood of my servants, the prophets, and the blood of all the servants of the Lord, at the hand of Jezebel.'"

And when Jehu was come to Jezreel, Jezebel heard of it; and she painted her face and tired her head and looked out at a window. And as Jehu entered in at the gate she said, "Had Zimri peace, who slew his master?"

And he lifted up his face to the window and said, "Who is on my side? Who?"

And there looked out to him two or three eunuchs.

And he said, "Throw her down."

So they threw her down, and some of her blood was sprinkled on the wall and on the horses, and he trode her under foot.

And when he was come in he did eat and drink, and said, "Go, see now this cursed woman and bury her, for she is a king's daughter."

And they went to bury her, but they found no more of her than the skull and the feet and the palms of her hands. Wherefore they came again and told him.

And he said, "This is the word of the Lord which he spake by his servant, Elijah the Tishbite, saying, 'In the portion of Jezreel shall dogs eat the flesh of Jezebel.'"

THE EUNUCHS SEIZE JEZEBEL

The words of Amos, who was among the herdmen of Tekoa, which he saw concerning Israel in the days of Uzziah, king of Judah, and in the days of Jeroboam, the son of Joash, king of Israel, two years before the earthquake.

And, behold, the Lord stood upon a wall made by a plumbline, with a plumbline in his hand.

And the Lord said unto me, "Amos, what seest thou?"

And I said, "A plumbline."

Then said the Lord, "Behold, I will set a plumbline in the midst of my people Israel. I will not again pass by them any more. And the high places of Isaac shall be desolate and the sanctuaries of Israel shall be laid waste; and I will rise against the house of Jeroboam with the sword."

Then Amaziah, the priest of Bethel, sent to Jeroboam, king of Israel, saying, "Amos hath conspired against thee in the midst of the house of Israel; the land is not able to bear all his words. For thus Amos saith: 'Jeroboam shall die by the sword, and Israel shall surely be led away captive out of their own land.'"

Also Amaziah said unto Amos, "O thou seer, go, flee thee away into the land of Judah, and there eat bread and prophesy there, but prophesy not again any more at Bethel, for it is the king's chapel, and it is the king's court."

Then answered Amos and said to Amaziah, "I was no prophet, neither was I a prophet's son; but I was an herdman and a gatherer of sycomore fruit. And the Lord took me as I followed the flock, and the Lord said unto me, 'Go, prophesy unto my people Israel.'"

Hear this word that the Lord hath spoken against you, O children of Israel, against the whole family which I brought up from the land of Egypt, saying:

"You only have I known of all the families of the earth. Therefore I will punish you for all your iniquities."

Can two walk together except they be agreed? Will a lion roar in the forest when he hath no prey? Will a young lion cry out of his den if he have taken nothing? Can a bird fall in a snare upon the earth, where no gin is for him? Shall one take up a snare from the earth and have taken nothing at all? Shall a trumpet be blown in the city and the people not be afraid? Shall there be evil in a city and the Lord hath not done it?

Surely the Lord God will do nothing but he revealeth his secret unto his servants, the prophets. The lion hath roared. Who will not fear? The Lord God hath spoken. Who can but prophesy?

Therefore the Lord, the God of hosts, the Lord, saith thus: "I hate, I despise your feast days, and I will not smell in your solemn assemblies. Though ye offer me burnt offerings and your meat offerings, I will not accept them; neither will I regard the peace offerings of your fat beasts. Take thou away from me the noise of thy songs; for I will not hear the melody of thy viols. But let judgment run down as waters, and righteousness as a mighty stream."

ISAIAH'S VISION OF SERAPHIMS

In the year that King Uzziah died I saw also the Lord sitting upon a throne, high and lifted up, and his train filled the temple. Above it stood the seraphims. Each one had six wings; with twain he covered his face, and with twain he covered his feet, and with twain he did fly.

And one cried unto another and said, "Holy, holy, holy is the Lord of hosts. The whole earth is full of his glory." And the posts of the door moved at the voice of him that cried, and the house was filled with smoke.

Then said I, "Woe is me! For I am undone, because I am a man of unclean lips and I dwell in the midst of a people of unclean lips, for mine eyes have seen the King, the Lord of hosts."

Then flew one of the seraphims unto me, having a live coal in his hand, which he had taken with the tongs from off the altar. And he laid it upon my mouth and said, "Lo, this hath touched thy lips, and thine iniquity is taken away and thy sin purged."

Also I heard the voice of the Lord, saying, "Whom shall I send, and who will go for us?"

Then said I, "Here am I; send me."

And he said, "Go, and tell this people, 'Hear ye indeed but understand not, and see ye indeed but perceive not. Make the heart of this people fat, and make their ears heavy, and shut their eyes; lest they see with their eyes, and hear with their ears, and understand with their heart, and convert, and be healed."

Then said I, "Lord, how long?"

And he answered, "Until the cities be wasted without inhabitant, and the houses without man, and the land be utterly desolate, and the Lord have removed men far away and there be a great forsaking in the midst of the land. But yet in it shall be a tenth, and it shall return and shall be eaten; as a teil tree, and as an oak, whose substance is in them when they cast their leaves: so the holy seed shall be the substance thereof."

Now it came to pass in the fourteenth year of King Hezekiah that Sennacherib, king of Assyria, came up against all the defenced cities of Judah and took them. And the king of Assyria sent Rabshakeh from Lachish to Jerusalem unto King Hezekiah with a great army. And he stood by the conduit of the upper pool in the highway of the fuller's field. Then came forth unto him Eliakim, Hilkiah's son, which was over the house, and Shebna the scribe, and Joah, Asaph's son, the recorder.

And Rabshakeh said unto them, "Say ye now to Hezekiah, 'Thus saith the great king, the king of Assyria: "What confidence is this wherein thou trustest? I say,"' sayest thou (but they are but vain words), ' "I have counsel and strength for war. Now on whom dost thou trust that thou rebellest against me? Lo, thou trustest in the staff of this broken reed, on Egypt, whereon, if a man lean, it will go into his hand and pierce it: so is Pharaoh, king of Egypt, to all that trust in him. But if thou say to me, 'We trust in the Lord, our God,' is it not he whose high places and whose altars Hezekiah hath taken away, and said to Judah and to Jerusalem, 'Ye shall worship before this altar'?"'

"Now therefore give pledges, I pray thee, to my master, the king of Assyria, and I will give thee two thousand horses if thou be able on thy part to set riders upon them. How then wilt thou turn away the face of one captain of the least of my master's servants and put thy trust on Egypt for chariots and for horsemen?

"And am I now come up without the Lord against this land to destroy it? The Lord said unto me, 'Go up against this land, and destroy it.'"

And it came to pass, when King Hezekiah heard it, that he rent his clothes and covered himself with sackcloth and went into the house of the Lord. And he sent Eliakim, who was over the household, and Shebna, the scribe, and the elders of the priests covered with sackcloth, unto Isaiah, the prophet, the son of Amoz. So the servants of King Hezekiah came to Isaiah.

And Isaiah said unto them, "Thus shall ye say unto your master: 'Thus saith the Lord, "Be not afraid of the words that thou hast heard, wherewith the servants of the king of Assyria have blasphemed me. Behold, I will send a blast upon him, and he shall hear a rumor and return to his own land; and I will cause him to fall by the sword in his own land."'"

Then the angel of the Lord went forth and smote in the camp of the Assyrians a hundred and fourscore and five thousand. And when they arose early in the morning, behold, they were all dead corpses. So Sennacherib, king of Assyria, departed, and went and returned and dwelt at Nineveh.

God is our refuge and strength,
 A very present help in trouble.
Therefore will not we fear, though the earth be removed,
 And though the mountains be carried into the midst of
  the sea,
Though the waters thereof roar and be troubled,
 Though the mountains shake with the swelling thereof.

There is a river, the streams whereof shall make glad the city
  of God,
 The holy place of the tabernacles of the most High.
Psalm 46 God is in the midst of her; she shall not be moved:
God shall help her, and that right early.
The heathen raged, the kingdoms were moved;
 He uttered his voice, the earth melted.
 The Lord of hosts is with us;
  The God of Jacob is our refuge.

He maketh wars to cease unto the end of the earth;
 He breaketh the bow and cutteth the spear in sunder;
 He burneth the chariot in the fire.
Be still, and know that I am God.

Moreover the Lord saith, "Because the daughters of Zion are haughty, and walk with stretched forth necks and wanton eyes, walking and mincing as they go, and making a tinkling with their feet, in that day the Lord will take away the bravery of their tinkling ornaments about their feet, and their cauls, and their round tires like the moon, the chains and the bracelets, and the mufflers, the bonnets, and the ornaments of the legs, and the headbands and the tablets and the earrings, the rings and nose jewels, the changeable suits of apparel and the mantles and the wimples and the crisping pins, the glasses and the fine linen, and the hoods and the veils.

"And it shall come to pass that instead of sweet smell there shall be stink; and instead of a girdle a rent; and instead of well set hair, baldness; and instead of a stomacher a girding of sackcloth; and burning instead of beauty."

And there shall come forth a rod out of the stem of Jesse, and a branch shall grow out of his roots; and the spirit of the Lord shall rest upon him, the spirit of wisdom and understanding, the spirit of counsel and might, the spirit of knowledge and of the fear of the Lord.

And shall make him of quick understanding in the fear of the Lord. And he shall not judge after the sight of his eyes, neither reprove after the hearing of his ears; but with righteousness shall he judge the poor and reprove with equity for the meek of the earth; and he shall smite the earth with the rod of his mouth, and with the breath of his lips shall he slay the wicked.

And righteousness shall be the girdle of his loins, and faithfulness the girdle of his reins. The wolf also shall dwell with the lamb, and the leopard shall lie down with the kid; and the calf and the young lion and the fatling together; and a little child shall lead them.

And the cow and the bear shall feed; their young ones shall lie down together; and the lion shall eat straw like the ox. And the sucking child shall play on the hole of the asp, and the weaned child shall put his hand on the cockatrice's den.

They shall not hurt nor destroy in all my holy mountain, for the earth shall be full of the knowledge of the Lord, as the waters cover the sea. And in that day there shall be a root of Jesse which shall stand for an ensign of the people. To it shall the Gentiles seek. And his rest shall be glorious.

As the hart panteth
    After the water brooks,
So panteth my soul
    After thee, O God!

My soul thirsteth for God,
    For the living God:
When shall I come and appear
    Before God?

My tears have been my meat
    Day and night,
While they continually say unto me,
    "Where is thy God?"

When I remember these things,
    I pour out my soul in me,
For I had gone with the multitude.
    I went with them to the house of God
With the voice of joy and praise,
    With a multitude that kept holyday.

Why art thou cast down, O my soul,
    And why art thou disquieted in me?
Hope thou in God, for I shall yet praise him:
    For the help of his countenance. O my God,

My soul is cast down within me.
    Therefore will I remember thee
From the land of Jordan, and of the Hermonites,
    From the hill Mizar.

Deep calleth unto deep
    At the noise of thy waterspouts:
All thy waves and thy billows
    Are gone over me.

Psalm 42

PSALMS
183

The words of Jeremiah, the son of Hilkiah, of the priests that were in Anathoth in the land of Benjamin:

Then the word of the Lord came unto me, saying, "Before I formed thee in the belly I knew thee; and before thou camest forth out of the womb I sanctified thee, and I ordained thee a prophet unto the nations."

Then said I, "Ah, Lord God! Behold, I cannot speak, for I am a child."

Jeremiah
Called to
Prophesy
JEREMIAH

But the Lord said unto me, "Say not, 'I am a child,' for thou shalt go to all that I shall send thee, and whatsoever I command thee thou shalt speak. Be not afraid of their faces, for I am with thee to deliver thee," saith the Lord.

Then the Lord put forth his hand and touched my mouth. And the Lord said unto me, "Behold, I have put my words in thy mouth."

When I would comfort myself against sorrow, my heart is faint in me.

Behold, the voice of the cry of the daughter of my people because of them that dwell in a far country: "Is not the Lord in Zion? Is not her king in her? Why have they provoked me to anger with their graven images and with strange vanities?"

Lament For Zion JEREMIAH

The harvest is past, the summer is ended and we are not saved. For the hurt of the daughter of my people am I hurt; I am black; astonishment hath taken hold on me. Is there no balm in Gilead; is there no physician there? Why, then, is not the health of the daughter of my people recovered?

"Behold, the days come," saith the Lord, "that I will sow the house of Israel and the house of Judah with the seed of man and with the seed of beast. And it shall come to pass that, like as I have watched over them, to pluck up, and to break down, and to throw down, and to destroy, and to afflict, so will I watch over them, to build and to plant," saith the Lord.

"In those days they shall say no more, 'The fathers have eaten a sour grape, and the children's teeth are set on edge.' But every one shall die for his own iniquity: every man that eateth the sour grape, his teeth shall be set on edge.

"Behold, the days come," saith the Lord, "that I will make a new covenant with the house of Israel and with the house of Judah. Not according to the covenant that I made with their fathers in the day that I took them by the hand to bring them out of the land of Egypt, which my covenant they brake, although I was an husband unto them," saith the Lord, "but this shall be the covenant that I will make with the house of Israel.

"After those days," saith the Lord, "I will put my law in their inward parts and write it in their hearts and will be their God, and they shall be my people. And they shall teach no more every man his neighbour, and every man his brother, saying, 'Know the Lord,' for they shall all know me, from the least of them unto the greatest of them," saith the Lord, "for I will forgive their iniquity and I will remember their sin no more."

Thus saith the Lord, which giveth the sun for a light by day, and the ordinances of the moon and of the stars for a light by night, which divideth the sea when the waves thereof roar. The Lord of hosts is his name.

THE BABYLONIAN EXILE

And it came to pass in the ninth year of his reign, in the tenth month, in the tenth day of the month, that Nebuchadnezzar, king of Babylon, came, he and all his host, against Jerusalem and pitched against it. And they built forts against it round about. And the city was besieged unto the eleventh year of King Zedekiah.

And on the ninth day of the fourth month the famine prevailed in the city and there was no bread for the people of the land. And the city was broken up, and all the men of war fled by night by the way of the gate between two walls, which is by the king's garden.

Now the Chaldees were against the city round about, and the king went the way toward the plain. And the army of the Chaldees pursued after the king and overtook him in the plains of Jericho; and all his army were scattered from him. So they took the king and brought him up to the king of Babylon, to Riblah, and they gave judgment upon him. And they slew the sons of Zedekiah before his eyes, and put

Exile to
Babylon
II KINGS
187

out the eyes of Zedekiah, and bound him with fetters of brass, and carried him to Babylon.

And in the fifth month, on the seventh day of the month, which is the nineteenth year of King Nebuchadnezzar, king of Babylon, came Nebuzaradan, captain of the guard, a servant of the king of Babylon, unto Jerusalem. And he burnt the house of the Lord and the king's house and all the houses of Jerusalem, and every great man's house burnt he with fire. And all the army of the Chaldees that were with the captain of the guard brake down the walls of Jerusalem round about.

Now the rest of the people that were left in the city, and the fugitives that fell away to the king of Babylon, with the remnant of the multitude, did Nebuzaradan, the captain of the guard, carry away. But the captain of the guard left of the poor of the land to be vinedressers and husbandmen.

And as for the people that remained in the land of Judah, whom Nebuchadnezzar, king of Babylon, had left, even over them he made Gedaliah, the son of Ahikam, the son of Shaphan, ruler.

The word of the Lord came expressly unto Ezekiel, the priest, the son of Buzi, in the land of the Chaldeans by the river Chebar.

For thus saith the Lord God, "Behold, I, even I, will both search my sheep and seek them out. As a shepherd seeketh out his flock in the day that he is among his sheep that are scattered, so will I seek out my sheep and will deliver them out of all places where they have been scattered in the cloudy and dark day. And I will bring them out from the people, and gather them from the countries, and will bring them to their own land and feed them upon the mountains of Israel by the rivers and in all the inhabited places of the country.

"I will feed them in a good pasture, and upon the high mountains of Israel shall their fold be: there shall they lie in a good fold, and in a fat pasture shall they feed upon the mountains of Israel. I will feed my flock, and I will cause them to lie down," saith the Lord God. "I will seek that which was lost and bring again that which was driven away, and will bind up that which was broken, and will strengthen that which was sick.

"And I will set up one shepherd over them, and he shall feed them, even my servant David; he shall feed them and he shall be their shepherd. And I, the Lord, will be their God, and my servant David a prince among them; I, the Lord, have spoken it.

"And I will make with them a covenant of peace, and will cause the evil beasts to cease out of the land; and they shall dwell safely in the wilderness and sleep in the woods.

And I will make them and the places round about my hill a blessing; and I will cause the shower to come down in his season; there shall be showers of blessing. And the tree of the field shall yield her fruit, and the earth shall yield her increase, and they shall be safe in their land and shall know that I am the Lord, when I have broken the bands of their yoke and delivered them out of the hand of those that served themselves of them.

"And they shall no more be a prey to the heathen, neither shall the beast of the land devour them; but they shall dwell safely and none shall make them afraid. And I will raise up for them a plant of renown, and they shall be no more consumed with hunger in the land, neither bear the shame of the heathen any more.

"Thus shall they know that I, the Lord, their God, am with them, and that they, even the house of Israel, are my people," saith the Lord God.

"And ye, my flock, the flock of my pasture, are men, and I am your God," saith the Lord God.

The hand of the Lord was upon me and carried me out in the spirit of the Lord and set me down in the midst of the valley which was full of bones, and caused me to pass by them round about. And, behold, there were very many in the open valley, and, lo, they were very dry.

And he said unto me, "Son of man, can these bones live?"

Vision of Dry Bones
EZEKIEL

And I answered, "O Lord God, thou knowest."

Again he said unto me, "Prophesy upon these bones, and say unto them, 'O ye dry bones, hear the word of the Lord.'"

Thus saith the Lord God unto these bones: "Behold, I will cause breath to enter into you, and ye shall live, and I will lay sinews upon you and will bring up flesh upon you, and cover you with skin, and put breath in you, and ye shall live; and ye shall know that I am the Lord."

So I prophesied as I was commanded, and as I prophesied, there was a noise and, behold, a shaking, and the bones came together, bone to his bone. And when I beheld, lo, the sinews and the flesh came up upon them, and the skin covered them above, but there was no breath in them.

Then said he unto me, "Prophesy unto the wind, prophesy, son of man, and say to the wind, 'Thus saith the Lord God: "Come from the four winds, O breath, and breathe upon these slain, that they may live."'"

So I prophesied as he commanded me, and the breath came into them, and they lived and stood up upon their feet, an exceeding great army.

Then he said unto me, "Son of man, these bones are the whole house of Israel. 'Behold,' they say, 'our bones are dried, and our hope is lost; we are cut off for our parts.'

"Therefore prophesy and say unto them, 'Thus saith the Lord God; "Behold, O my people, I will open your graves and cause you to come up out of your graves and bring you into the land of Israel. And ye shall know that I am the Lord when I have opened your graves, O my people, and brought you up out of your graves, and shall put my spirit in you, and ye shall live, and I shall place you in your own land. Then shall ye know that I, the Lord, hath spoken it, and performed it,"'" saith the Lord.

THE CHILDREN OF ISRAEL WEEP BY THE WATERS OF BABYLON

By the waters of Babylon,
    There we sat down, yea, we wept,
When we remembered Zion.
Upon the willows in the midst thereof,
    We hanged our harps.
For there they that carried us away captive
    Required of us a song.
And they that wasted us required of us mirth, saying,
    "Sing us one of the songs of Zion!"

How shall we sing the Lord's song
    In a strange land?
If I forget thee, O Jerusalem,
    Let my right hand forget her cunning!
Let my tongue cleave to the roof of my mouth
    If I do not remember thee,
If I prefer not Jerusalem
    Above my chief joy!

Remember, O Lord, the children of Edom
    In the day of Jerusalem,
Who said, "Rase it! Rase it!
    Even to the foundation thereof!"
O daughter of Babylon, who art to be destroyed,
    Happy shall he be that rewardeth thee
    As thou hast served us!
Happy shall he be that taketh and dasheth
    Thy little ones against the stones!

ow there was a day when the sons of God came to present themselves before the Lord, and Satan came also among them.

And the Lord said unto Satan, "Whence comest thou?"

Then Satan answered the Lord and said, "From going to and fro in the earth, and from walking up and down in it."

And the Lord said unto Satan, "Hast thou considered my servant Job, that there is none like him in the earth, a perfect and an upright man, one that feareth God and escheweth evil?"

Then Satan answered the Lord and said, "Doth Job fear God for nought? Hast not thou made an hedge about him, and about his house, and about all that he hath on every side? Thou hast blessed the work of his hands, and his substance is increased in the land. But put forth thine hand now and touch all that he hath, and he will curse thee to thy face."

And the Lord said unto Satan, "Behold, all that he hath is in thy power; only upon himself put not forth thine hand."

So Satan went forth from the presence of the Lord.

And there was a day when a messenger came unto Job and said, "The oxen were plowing and the asses feeding beside them, and the Sabeans fell upon them and took them away. Yea, they have slain the servants with the edge of the sword, and I only am escaped alone to tell thee."

While he was yet speaking there came also another and said, "The fire of God is fallen from heaven and hath burned up the sheep and the servants and consumed them, and I only am escaped alone to tell thee."

JOB AND HIS THREE FRIENDS

While he was yet speaking there came also another and said, "The Chaldeans made out three bands and fell upon the camels and have carried them away, yea, and slain the servants with the edge of the sword, and I only am escaped alone to tell thee."

While he was yet speaking there came also another and said, "Thy sons and thy daughters were eating and drinking wine in their eldest brother's house and, behold, there came a great wind from the wilderness and smote the four corners of the house, and it fell upon the young men and they are dead, and I only am escaped alone to tell thee."

Then Job arose and rent his mantle, and shaved his head, and fell down upon the ground and worshipped, and said, "Naked came I out of my mother's womb, and naked shall I return thither. The Lord gave, and the Lord hath taken away, blessed be the name of the Lord!"

In all this Job sinned not nor charged God foolishly.

Again there was a day when the sons of God came to present themselves before the Lord, and Satan came also among them to present himself before the Lord.

And the Lord said unto Satan, "From whence comest thou?"

And Satan answered the Lord and said, "From going to and fro in the earth, and from walking up and down in it."

And the Lord said unto Satan, "Hast thou considered my servant Job? He holdeth fast his integrity, although thou movedst me against him, to destroy him without cause."

And Satan answered the Lord and said, "Skin for skin, yea, all that a man hath will he give for his life. But put forth thine hand now and touch his bone and his flesh, and he will curse thee to thy face."

And the Lord said unto Satan, "Behold, he is in thine hand, but save his life."

So went Satan forth from the presence of the Lord and smote Job with sore boils from the sole of his foot unto his crown. And Job took him a potsherd to scrape himself withal, and he sat down among the ashes.

Then said his wife unto him, "Dost thou still retain thine integrity? Curse God, and die."

But he said unto her, "Thou speakest as one of the foolish women speaketh. What? Shall we receive good at the hand of God, and shall we not receive evil?"

In all this did not Job sin with his lips.

Now when Job's three friends heard of all this evil that was come upon him they came every one from his own place: Eliphaz the Temanite, and Bildad the Shuhite, and Zophar the Naamathite. For they had made an appointment together to come to mourn with him and to comfort him.

And when they lifted up their eyes afar off and knew him not, they lifted up their voice and wept; and they rent every one his mantle and sprinkled dust upon their heads toward heaven. So they sat down with him upon the ground seven days and seven nights, and none spake a word unto him, for they saw that his grief was very great.

After this opened Job his mouth, and Job spake and said, "Let the day perish wherein I was born. Why died I not from the womb? Why did I not give up the ghost when I came out of the belly? For my sighing cometh before I eat, and my roarings are poured out like the waters. For the thing which I greatly feared is come upon me and that which I was afraid of is come unto me."

Then Eliphaz the Temanite answered and said, "Behold, thou hast instructed many, and thou hast strengthened the weak hands. Thy words have upholden him that was falling, and thou hast strengthened the feeble knees. But now it is come upon thee and thou faintest; it toucheth thee and thou art troubled. Is not this thy fear, thy confidence, thy hope, and the uprightness of thy ways? Behold, happy is the man whom God correcteth; therefore despise not thou the chastening of the Almighty."

But Job answered and said, "Is there not an appointed time to man upon earth? Are not his days also like the days of an hireling? As a servant earnestly desireth the shadow, and as an hireling looketh for the reward of his work, so am I made to possesss months of vanity, and wearisome nights are appointed to me. When I lie down I say, 'When shall I arise, and the night be gone?' And I am full of tossings to and fro unto the dawning of the day.

"My flesh is clothed with worms and clods of dust; my skin is broken and become loathsome. My days are swifter than a weaver's shuttle, and are spent without hope.

"O remember that my life is wind: mine eye shall no more see good. The eye of him that hath seen me shall see me no more: thine eyes are upon me, and I am not.

"As the cloud is consumed and vanisheth away, so he that goeth down to the grave shall come up no more. He shall return no more to his house, neither shall his place know him any more. Therefore I will not refrain my mouth. I will speak in the anguish of my spirit. I will complain in the bitterness of my soul.

"Am I a sea, or a whale, that thou settest a watch over me? When I say, 'My bed shall comfort me, my couch shall ease my complaint,' then thou scarest me with dreams and terrifiest me through visions, so that my soul chooseth strangling, and death rather than my life. I loathe it. I would not live alway: let me alone, for my days are vanity.

"What is man that thou shouldest magnify him? And that thou shouldest set thine heart upon him? And that thou shouldest visit him every morning and try him every moment? How long wilt thou not depart from me nor let me alone till I swallow down my spittle?

"I have sinned. What shall I do unto thee, O thou preserver of men? Why hast thou set me as a mark against thee, so that I am a burden to myself? And why dost thou not pardon my transgression and take away mine iniquity? For now shall I sleep in the dust, and thou shalt seek me in the morning but I shall not be.

"Man that is born of a woman is of few days and full of trouble. He cometh forth like a flower and is cut down; he fleeth also as a shadow, and continueth not. And dost thou open thine eyes upon such an one and bringest me into judgment with thee?

"Who can bring a clean thing out of an unclean? Not one. Seeing his days are determined, the number of his months are with thee, thou hast appointed his bounds that he cannot pass. Turn from him, that he may rest, till he shall accomplish, as an hireling, his day.

"For there is hope of a tree, if it be cut down, that it will sprout again and that the tender branch thereof will not cease. Though the root thereof wax old in the earth, and the stock thereof die in the ground, yet through the scent of water it will bud and bring forth boughs like a plant. But man dieth and wasteth away; yea, man giveth up the ghost, and where is he?

"Know now that God hath overthrown me and hath compassed me with his net. Behold, I cry out of wrong but I am not heard. I cry aloud but there is no judgment.

"He hath fenced up my way that I cannot pass, and he hath set darkness in my paths. He hath stripped me of my glory and taken the crown from my head. He hath destroyed me on every side and I am gone, and mine hope hath he

removed like a tree. He hath also kindled his wrath against me, and he counteth me unto him as one of his enemies.

"Have pity upon me, have pity upon me, O ye, my friends, for the hand of God hath touched me.

"Oh that my words were now written! Oh that they were printed in a book, that they were graven with an iron pen and lead in the rock for ever! For I know that my redeemer liveth, and that he shall stand at the latter day upon the earth. And though after my skin worms destroy this body, yet in my flesh shall I see God, whom I shall see for myself, and mine eyes shall behold, and not another, though my reins be consumed within me.

"Oh that I knew where I might find him, that I might come even to his seat! I would know the words which he would answer me, and understand what he would say unto me."

Then the Lord answered Job out of the whirlwind and said, "Who is this that darkeneth counsel by words without knowledge? Gird up now thy loins like a man, for I will demand of thee, and answer thou me. Where wast thou when I laid the foundations of the earth? Declare, if thou hast understanding.

"Who hath laid the measures thereof, if thou knowest? Or who hath stretched the line upon it? Whereupon are the foundations thereof fastened? Or who laid the corner stone thereof, when the morning stars sang together, and all the sons of God shouted for joy?

"Canst thou bind the sweet influences of Pleiades or loose the bands of Orion? Canst thou bring forth Mazzaroth in his season? Or canst thou guide Arcturus with his sons? Knowest thou the ordinances of heaven? Canst thou set the dominion thereof in the earth?"

Then Job answered the Lord and said, "I know that thou canst do everything and that no thought can be withholden from thee. Who is he that hideth counsel without knowledge? Therefore have I uttered that I understood not, things too wonderful for me, which I knew not.

"Hear, I beseech thee, and I will speak; I will demand of thee, and declare thou unto me. I have heard of thee by the hearing of the ear, but now mine eye seeth thee. Wherefore I abhor myself and repent in dust and ashes."

"Comfort ye, comfort ye my people," saith your God. "Speak ye comfortably to Jerusalem, and cry unto her, that her warfare is accomplished, that her iniquity is pardoned, for she hath received of the Lord's hand double for all her sins."

The voice of him that crieth in the wilderness: "Prepare ye the way of the Lord, make straight in the desert a highway for our God. Every valley shall be exalted and every mountain and hill shall be made low; and the crooked shall be made straight and the rough places plain. And the glory of the Lord shall be revealed, and all flesh shall see it together, for the mouth of the Lord hath spoken it."

The voice said, "Cry."

And he said, "What shall I cry?" All flesh is grass, and all the goodliness thereof is as the flower of the field: the grass withereth, the flower fadeth; because the spirit of the Lord bloweth upon it. Surely the people is grass. The grass withereth, the flower fadeth, but the word of our God shall stand for ever.

O Zion, that bringest good tidings, get thee up into the high mountain. O Jerusalem, that bringest good tidings, lift up thy voice with strength, lift it up, be not afraid. Say unto the cities of Judah, "Behold your God!"

Behold, the Lord God will come with strong hand, and his arm shall rule for him. Behold, his reward is with him and his work before him. He shall feed his flock like a shepherd; he shall gather the lambs with his arm, and carry them in his bosom, and shall gently lead those that are with young.

Who hath measured the waters in the hollow of his hand, and meted out heaven with the span, and comprehended the dust of the earth in a measure, and weighed the mountains in scales, and the hills in a balance? Who hath directed the spirit of the Lord or, being his counsellor, hath taught him? With whom took he counsel, and who instructed him, and taught him in the path of judgment, and taught him knowledge, and shewed to him the way of understanding?

Behold, the nations are as a drop of a bucket and are counted as the small dust of the balance. Behold, he taketh up the isles as a very little thing.

Hast thou not known? Hast thou not heard that the everlasting God, the Lord, the Creator of the ends of the earth, fainteth not, neither is weary? There is no searching of his understanding.

He giveth power to the faint; and to them that have no might he increaseth strength. Even the youths shall faint and be weary, and the young men shall utterly fall, but they that wait upon the Lord shall renew their strength; they shall mount up with wings as eagles; they shall run and not be weary; and they shall walk and not faint.

Who hath believed our report? And to whom is the arm of the Lord revealed? For he shall grow up before him as a tender plant and as a root out of a dry ground: he hath no form nor comeliness; and when we shall see him there is no beauty that we should desire him.

He is despised and rejected of men, a man of sorrows, and acquainted with grief; and we hid, as it were, our faces from him; he was despised and we esteemed him not.

Surely he hath borne our griefs and carried our sorrows, yet we did esteem him stricken, smitten of God, and afflicted.

But he was wounded for our transgressions, he was bruised for our iniquities: the chastisement of our peace was upon him; and with his stripes we are healed. All we, like sheep, have gone astray; we have turned every one to his own way, and the Lord hath laid on him the iniquity of us all.

He was oppressed and he was afflicted, yet he opened not his mouth. He is brought as a lamb to the slaughter, and as a sheep before her shearers is dumb, so he openeth not his mouth. He was taken from prison and from judgment: and who shall declare his generation? For he was cut off out of the land of the living; for the transgression of my people was he stricken.

And he made his grave with the wicked, and with the rich in his death; because he had done no violence, neither was any deceit in his mouth. Yet it pleased the Lord to bruise him; he hath put him to grief. When thou shall make his soul an offering for sin, he shall see his seed, he shall prolong his days, and the pleasure of the Lord shall prosper in his hand.

He shall see of the travail of his soul and shall be satisfied; by his knowledge shall my righteous servant justify many, for he shall bear their iniquities. Therefore will I

divide him a portion with the great, and he shall divide the spoil with the strong, because he hath poured out his soul unto death; and he was numbered with the transgressors; and he bare the sin of many and made intercession for the transgressors.

Ho, every one that thirsteth, come ye to the waters; and he that hath no money, come ye, buy and eat; yea, come, buy wine and milk without money and without price.

Wherefore do ye spend money for that which is not bread, and your labour for that which satisfieth not? Hearken diligently unto me, and eat ye that which is good, and let your soul delight itself in fatness.

Incline your ear and come unto me: hear, and your soul shall live. Seek ye the Lord while he may be found, call ye upon him while he is near.

Let the wicked forsake his way and the unrighteous man his thoughts, and let him return unto the Lord, and he will have mercy upon him; and to our God, for he will

abundantly pardon.

"For my thoughts are not your thoughts, neither are your ways my ways," saith the Lord. "For as the heavens are higher than the earth, so are my ways higher than your ways, and my thoughts than your thoughts. For as the rain cometh down, and the snow from heaven, and returneth not thither but watereth the earth, and maketh it bring forth and bud, that it may give seed to the sower and bread to the eater, so shall my word be that goeth forth out of my mouth. It shall not return unto me void, but it shall accomplish that which I please, and it shall prosper in the thing whereto I sent it.

"For ye shall go out with joy and be led forth with peace: the mountains and the hills shall break forth before you into singing, and all the trees of the field shall clap their hands.

"Instead of the thorn shall come up the fir tree, and instead of the brier shall come up the myrtle tree: and it shall be to the Lord for a name, for an everlasting sign that shall not be cut off."

ow in the first year of Cyrus, king of Persia, that the word of the Lord by the mouth of Jeremiah might be fulfilled, the Lord stirred up the spirit of Cyrus, king of Persia, that he made a proclamation throughout all his kingdom and put it also in writing, saying,

"Thus saith Cyrus, king of Persia: The Lord God of heaven hath given me all the kingdoms of the earth; and he hath charged me to build him an house at Jerusalem, which is in Judah.

Decree of Cyrus

EZRA

"Who is there among you of all his people? His God be with him, and let him go up to Jerusalem, which is in Judah, and build the house of the Lord God of Israel (he is the God) which is in Jerusalem.

"And whosoever remaineth in any place where he sojourneth, let the men of his place help him with silver and with gold and with goods and with beasts, beside the freewill offering for the house of God that is in Jerusalem."

Then rose up the chief of the fathers of Judah and Benjamin, and the priests and the Levites, with all them whose spirit God had raised, to go up to build the house of the Lord which is in Jerusalem.

And when the seventh month was come, and the children of Israel were in the cities, the people gathered themselves together as one man to Jerusalem.

THE RESTORATION

When the Lord turned again the captivity of Zion,
  We were like them that dream.
Then was our mouth filled with laughter,
  And our tongue with singing:

Then said they among the heathen,
  "The Lord hath done great things for them;"
The Lord hath done great things for us
  Whereof we are glad.

Turn again our captivity, O Lord,
  As the streams in the south.
They that sow in tears
  Shall reap in joy.

He that goeth forth and weepeth,
  Bearing precious seed,
Shall doubtless come again with rejoicing,
  Bringing his sheaves with him.

Psalm 126

PSALMS

209

The words of Nehemiah, the son of Hachaliah:

And it came to pass in the month Chisleu, in the twentieth year, as I was in Shushan, the palace, that Hanani, one of my brethren, came, he and certain men of Judah; and I asked them concerning the Jews that had escaped, which were left of the captivity, and concerning Jerusalem.

And they said unto me, "The remnant that are left of the captivity there in the province are in great affliction and reproach. The wall of Jerusalem also is broken down, and the gates thereof are burned with fire." And it came to pass, when I heard these words, that I sat down and wept, and mourned certain days, and fasted, and prayed before the God of heaven.

And it came to pass in the month Nisan, in the twentieth year of Artaxerxes, the king, that wine was before him. And I took up the wine and gave it unto the king. Now I had not been beforetime sad in his presence.

Wherefore the king said unto me, "Why is thy countenance sad, seeing thou art not sick? This is nothing else but sorrow of heart."

Then I was very sore afraid and said unto the king, "Let the king live for ever. Why should not my countenance be sad when the city, the place of my fathers' sepulchres, lieth waste, and the gates thereof are consumed with fire?"

Then the king said unto me, "For what dost thou make request?"

So I prayed to the God of heaven. And I said unto the king, "If it please the king, and if thy servant have found favour in thy sight, that thou wouldest send me unto Judah, unto the city of my fathers' sepulchres, that I may build it."

And the king said unto me (the queen also sitting by him), "For how long shall thy journey be? And when wilt thou return?"

So it pleased the king to send me; and I set him a time.

Moreover I said unto the king, "If it please the king, let letters be given me to the governors beyond the river, that they may convey me over till I come into Judah; and a letter unto Asaph, the keeper of the king's forest, that he may give me timber to make beams for the gates of the palace which appertained to the house, and for the wall of the city, and for the house that I shall enter into."

And the king granted me, according to the good hand of my God upon me. Then I came to the governors beyond the river and gave them the king's letters. Now the king had

sent captains of the army and horsemen with me.

So I came to Jerusalem and was there three days. And I arose in the night, I and some few men with me; neither told I any man what my God had put in my heart to do at Jerusalem; neither was there any beast with me, save the beast that I rode upon.

And I went out by night by the gate of the valley, even before the dragon well, and to the dung port, and viewed the walls of Jerusalem, which were broken down, and the gates thereof were consumed with fire. Then I went on to the gate of the fountain, and to the king's pool, but there was no place for the beast that was under me to pass. Then went I up in the night by the brook, and viewed the wall, and turned back, and entered by the gate of the valley, and so returned.

And the rulers knew not whither I went or what I did; neither had I as yet told it to the Jews, nor to the priests, nor to the nobles, nor to the rulers, nor to the rest that did the work.

Then said I unto them, "Ye see the distress that we are in, how Jerusalem lieth waste and the gates thereof are burned with fire. Come, and let us build up the wall of Jerusalem, that we be no more a reproach."

Now it came to pass, when the wall was built and I had set up the doors, and the porters and the singers and the Levites were appointed, that I gave my brother Hanani, and Hananiah, the ruler of the palace, charge over Jerusalem, for he was a faithful man and feared God above many.

And I said unto them, "Let not the gates of Jerusalem be opened until the sun be hot; and while they stand by, let them shut the doors and bar them. And appoint watches of the inhabitants of Jerusalem, every one in his watch, and every one to be over against his house."

NEHEMIAH VIEWS THE BROKEN WALLS OF JERUSALEM

I will lift up mine eyes unto the hills,
  From whence cometh my help.
My help cometh from the Lord,
  Which made heaven and earth.

He will not suffer thy foot to be moved;
  He that keepeth thee will not slumber.
Behold, he shall neither slumber nor sleep,
  That keepeth Israel.

The Lord is thy keeper;
  The Lord is thy shade upon thy right hand.
The sun shall not smite thee by day
  Nor the moon by night.

The Lord shall preserve thee from all evil:
  He shall preserve thy soul.
The Lord shall preserve thy going out and thy coming in
  From this time forth and even for evermore.

Psalm 121

PSALMS

In those days, when the king Ahasuerus sat on the throne of his kingdom, which was in Shushan, the palace, the king made a feast unto all the people that were present. Also Vashti the queen made a feast for the women. When the heart of the king was merry with wine, he commanded the seven chamberlains to bring Vashti the queen before the king with the crown royal, to shew the people and the princes her beauty. But the queen Vashti refused to come at the king's commandment, therefore, was the king very wroth. Then the king said to the wise men,

"What shall we do unto the queen Vashti because she hath not performed the commandment of the king?" And Memucan answered, "If it please the king, let there go a royal commandment from him, and let it be written among the laws of the Persians and the Medes, that it be not altered, that Vashti come no more before the king, and let the king give her royal estate unto another that is better than she."

And the saying pleased the king. And the king did according to the word of Memucan.

Then said the king's servants that ministered unto him, "Let there be fair young virgins sought for the king. And let the maiden which pleaseth the king be queen instead of Vashti."

And the thing pleased the king; and he did so.

Now in Shushan, the palace, there was a certain Jew, whose name was Mordecai, who had been carried away from Jerusalem with the captivity. And he brought up Esther, his uncle's daughter; for she had neither father nor mother, and the maid was fair and beautiful.

ESTHER GOES TO PLEAD WITH THE KING

And the king loved Esther above all the women, and she obtained grace and favour in his sight more than all the virgins; so that he set the royal crown upon her head, and made her queen instead of Vashti.

In those days, while Mordecai sat in the king's gate, two of the king's chamberlains, Bigthan and Teresh, of those which kept the door, were wroth, and sought to lay hand on the king Ahasuerus. And the thing was known to Mordecai, who told it unto Esther the queen; and Esther certified the king thereof in Mordecai's name. And when inquisition was made of the matter, they were both hanged on a tree; and it was written in the book of the chronicles before the king.

After these things did King Ahasuerus promote Haman and set his seat above all the princes that were with him. And all the king's servants that were in the king's gate, bowed, and reverenced Haman: for the king had so commanded concerning him. But Mordecai bowed not, nor did him reverence.

And when Haman saw that Mordecai bowed not, nor did him reverence, then was Haman full of wrath. Wherefore Haman sought to destroy all the Jews that were throughout the whole kingdom of Ahasuerus, even the people of Mordecai. And Haman said unto King Ahasuerus,

"There is a certain people scattered abroad and dispersed among the people in all the provinces of thy kingdom; and their laws are diverse from all people; neither keep they the king's laws. Therefore it is not for the king's profit to suffer them. If it please the king, let it be written that they may be destroyed."

And the king took his ring from his hand and gave it unto Haman. And the letters were sent by posts into all the king's provinces, to destroy, to kill, and to cause to perish, all Jews, both young and old, little children and women, in one day, even upon the thirteenth day of the twelfth month, which is the month Adar, and to take the spoil of them for a prey.

When Mordecai perceived all that was done, Mordecai rent his clothes, and put on sackcloth with ashes, and went out into the midst of the city, and cried with a loud and a bitter cry; and came even before the king's gate; for none might enter into the king's gate clothed with sackcloth.

So Esther's maids and her chamberlains came and told it her. Then was the queen exceedingly grieved; and she sent raiment to clothe Mordecai, and to take away his sackcloth from him; but he received it not.

Then called Esther for Hatach, one of the king's chamberlains, whom he had appointed to attend upon her, and gave him a commandment to Mordecai, to know what it was, and why it was. So Hatach went forth to Mordecai unto the street of the city, which was before the king's gate.

And Mordecai told him of all that had happened unto him; also he gave him the copy of the writing of the decree that was given at Shushan to destroy them, to shew it unto Esther, and to charge her that she should go in unto the king, to make supplication unto him for her people.

And Hatach came and told Esther the words of Mordecai. Again Esther spake unto Hatach, and gave him commandment unto Mordecai, "All the king's servants do know that whosoever, whether man or woman, shall come unto the king into the inner court, who is not called, there is one law of his to put him to death, except such to whom the king shall hold out the golden sceptre."

And they told to Mordecai Esther's words. Then Mordecai commanded to answer Esther, "Who knoweth whether thou art come to the kingdom for such a time as this?"

Then Esther bade them return Mordecai this answer, "I will go in unto the king, which is not according to the law;

HAMAN SEES MORDECAI IN THE KING'S GATE

and if I perish, I perish."

Now it came to pass on the third day, that Esther put on her royal apparel, and stood in the inner court of the king's house, and when the king saw Esther the queen standing in the court, he held out to Esther the golden sceptre. So Esther drew near, and touched the top of the sceptre.

Then said the king unto her, "What wilt thou, Queen Esther? And what is thy request? It shall be even given thee to the half of the kingdom."

And Esther answered, "If it seem good unto the king, let the king and Haman come this day unto the banquet that I have prepared for him."

Then went Haman forth that day joyful and with a glad heart; but when Haman saw Mordecai in the king's gate, that he stood not up, nor moved for him, he was full of indignation. When he came home, he sent and called for his friends, and Zeresh his wife. And Haman told them the king had promoted him.

Haman said, "Yet all this availeth me nothing, so long as I see Mordecai the Jew sitting at the king's gate."

Then said Zeresh his wife and all his friends unto him, "Let a gallows be made of fifty cubits high, and tomorrow speak thou unto the king that Mordecai may be hanged thereon." And Haman caused the gallows to be made.

On that night could not the king sleep, and he commanded to bring the book of records of the chronicles; and they were read before the king. And it was found written, that Mordecai had told of Bigthan and Teresh, two of the king's chamberlains, the keepers of the door, who sought to lay hand on the king Ahasuerus.

And the king said, "What honour and dignity hath been done to Mordecai for this?"

Then said the king's servants, "There is nothing done for him."

And the king said, "Who is in the court?"

Now Haman was come into the outward court of the king's house, to speak unto the king to hang Mordecai on the gallows that he had prepared for him. And the king's servants said unto him,

"Behold, Haman standeth in the court." And the king said, "Let him come in."

So Haman came in. And the king said unto him,

"What shall be done unto the man whom the king delighteth to honour?" Now Haman thought in his heart, "To whom would the king delight to do honour more than to myself?"

And Haman answered,

"Let the royal apparel be brought which the king useth to wear, and the horse that the king rideth upon, and the crown royal which is set upon his head, and bring him on horseback through the street of the city, and proclaim before him."

Then the king said to Haman,

"Make haste, and take the apparel and the horse, as thou hast said, and do even so to Mordecai the Jew, that sitteth at the king's gate."

The king and Haman came to banquet with Esther the queen. And the king said, "What is thy petition, Queen Esther? and it shall be granted thee."

Then Esther the queen answered and said, "If I have found favour in thy sight, O king, and if it please the king, let my life be given me at my petition, and my people at my request. For we are sold, I and my people, to be destroyed, to be slain, and to perish. But if we had been sold for bondmen and bondwomen, I had held my tongue, although the enemy could not countervail the king's damage."

Then the king Ahasuerus answered and said unto Esther the queen, "Who is he, and where is he, that durst presume in his heart to do so?"

And Esther said, "The adversary and enemy is this wicked Haman."

Then Haman was afraid before the king and the queen.

And Harbonah, one of the chamberlains, said before the king, "Behold also, the gallows fifty cubits high, which Haman had made for Mordecai, who had spoken good for the king, standeth in the house of Haman."

Then the king said, "Hang him thereon."

So they hanged Haman on the gallows that he had prepared for Mordecai. Then was the king's wrath pacified.

And the king took off his ring, which he had taken from Haman, and gave it unto Mordecai. And Esther set Mordecai over the house of Haman.

And Esther spake yet again before the king, and fell down at his feet, and besought him with tears to put away the mischief of Haman and his device that he had devised against the Jews.

Wherein the king granted the Jews which were in every city to gather themselves together, and to stand for their life.

When the judges ruled, there was a famine in the land. And a certain man of Bethlehem-judah went to sojourn in the country of Moab, he and his wife and his two sons. And the name of the man was Elimelech, and the name of his wife Naomi, and the name of his two sons Mahlon and Chilion, Ephrathites of Bethlehem-judah. And they came into the country of Moab and continued there. And Elimelech, Naomi's husband, died; and she was left, and her two sons. And they took them wives of the women of Moab; the name of the one was Orpah and the name of the other Ruth. And they dwelled there about ten years.

And Mahlon and Chilion died also, both of them; and the woman was left of her two sons and her husband. Then she arose with her daughters-in-law, that she might return from the country of Moab, for she had heard in the country of Moab how that the Lord had visited his people in giving them bread. Wherefore she went forth out of the place where she was, and her two daughters-in-law with her; and they went on the way to return unto the land of Judah.

And Naomi said unto her two daughters-in-law, "Go, return each to her mother's house. The Lord deal kindly with you, as ye have dealt with the dead, and with me." Then she kissed them, and they lifted up their voice and wept.

And they said unto her, "Surely we will return with thee unto thy people."

And Naomi said, "Turn again, my daughters. Why will ye go with me?"

And they lifted up their voice and wept again. And Orpah kissed her mother-in-law, but Ruth clave unto her.

And Naomi said, "Behold, thy sister-in-law is gone back unto her people and unto her gods; return thou after thy sister-in-law."

And Ruth said, "Entreat me not to leave thee or to return from following after thee, for whither thou goest I will go, and where thou lodgest I will lodge. Thy people shall be my people, and thy God my God. Where thou diest will I die, and there will I be buried. The Lord do so to me, and more also, if aught but death part thee and me."

When Naomi saw that Ruth was stedfastly minded to go with her, then she left speaking unto her. So they two went until they came to Bethlehem.

And Naomi had a kinsman of her husband's, a mighty man of wealth, and his name was Boaz.

And Ruth the Moabitess said unto Naomi, "Let me now go to the field and glean ears of corn after him in whose sight I shall find grace."

And Naomi said unto her, "Go, my daughter."

And she went, and came, and gleaned in the field after the reapers; and her hap was to light on a part of the field belonging unto Boaz.

And, behold, Boaz came from Bethlehem, and said unto the reapers, "Whose damsel is this?"

And the servant that was set over the reapers answered and said, "It is the Moabitish damsel that came back with Naomi out of the country of Moab."

Then said Boaz unto Ruth, "Go not to glean in another field, neither go from hence, but abide here fast by my maidens."

Then she fell on her face and bowed herself to the ground and said unto him, "Why have I found grace in thine eyes, that thou shouldest take knowledge of me, seeing I am a stranger?"

And Boaz answered and said unto her, "It hath fully been shewed me all that thou hast done unto thy mother-in-law since the death of thine husband. At mealtime come thou hither, and eat of the bread and dip thy morsel in the vinegar."

And she sat beside the reapers; and he reached her parched corn, and she did eat, and was sufficed, and left.

And when she was risen up to glean, Boaz commanded his young men, saying, "Let her glean even among the sheaves, and let fall also some of the handfuls of purpose for her, and leave them that she may glean them."

So she gleaned in the field until even, and beat out that she had gleaned. And it was about an ephah of barley. And she took it up and went into the city.

And her mother-in-law said unto her, "Where hast thou gleaned today? And where wroughtest thou. Blessed be he that did take knowledge of thee."

And she shewed her mother-in-law with whom she had wrought, and said, "The man's name with whom I wrought today is Boaz."

Then Naomi, her mother-in-law, said unto her, "My daughter, shall I not seek rest for thee, that it may be well with thee? And now is not Boaz of our kindred, with whose maidens thou wast? Behold, he winnoweth barley to night in the threshingfloor. Wash thyself therefore, and anoint thee and put thy raiment upon thee, and get thee down to the floor; but make not thyself known unto the man until he shall have done eating and drinking. And it shall be, when he lieth down, that thou shalt mark the place where he shall lie, and thou shalt go in and uncover his feet and lay thee down; and he will tell thee what thou shalt do."

And Ruth said unto her, "All that thou sayest unto me I will do." And she went down unto the floor and did according to all that her mother-in-law bade her. And it came to pass at midnight that the man was afraid, and turned himself, and, behold, a woman lay at his feet.

And he said, "Who art thou?"

And she answered, "I am Ruth, thine handmaid; spread therefore thy skirt over thine handmaid, for thou art a near kinsman."

And he said, "Blessed be thou of the Lord, my daughter, for thou hast shewed more kindness in the latter end than at the beginning, inasmuch as thou followedst not young men, whether poor or rich. And now, my daughter, fear not; I will do to thee all that thou requirest, for all the city of my people doth know that thou art a virtuous woman. And now it is true that I am thy near kinsman; howbeit, there is a kinsman nearer than I. Tarry this night, and it shall be in the morning that if he will perform unto thee the part of a kinsman, well; let him do the kinsman's part. But if he will not do the part of a kinsman to thee, then will I do the part of a kinsman to thee, as the Lord liveth. Lie down until the morning."

And she lay at his feet until the morning. And she rose up before one could know another.

And he said, "Let it not be known that a woman came into the floor." Also he said, "Bring the veil that thou hast upon thee, and hold it."

And when she held it he measured six measures of barley and laid it on her; and she went into the city.

And when she came to her mother-in-law, Naomi said, "Who art thou, my daughter?"

And she told her all that the man had done to her. And she said, "These six measures of barley gave he me, for he said to me, 'Go not empty unto thy mother-in-law.'"

Then Naomi said, "Sit still, my daughter, until thou know how the matter will fall, for the man will not be in rest until he have finished the thing this day."

Then went Boaz up to the gate and sat him down there, and, behold, the kinsman of whom Boaz spake came by, unto whom he said, "Ho, such a one! Turn aside, sit down here." And he turned aside and sat down.

And Boaz took ten men of the elders of the city and said, "Sit ye down here." And they sat down.

And he said unto the kinsman, "Naomi, that is come again out of the country of Moab, selleth a parcel of land which was our brother Elimelech's. And I thought to advertise thee, saying, 'Buy it before the inhabitants, and before the elders of my people.' If thou wilt redeem it, redeem it; but if thou wilt not redeem it, then tell me, that I may know, for there is none to redeem it beside thee; and I am after thee."

And the kinsman said, "I will redeem it."

Then said Boaz, "What day thou buyest the field of the hand of Naomi, thou must buy it also of Ruth the Moabitess, the wife of the dead, to raise up the name of the dead upon his inheritance."

And the kinsman said, "I cannot redeem it for myself, lest I mar mine own inheritance. Redeem thou my right to thyself, for I cannot redeem it."

Now this was the manner in former time in Israel concerning redeeming and concerning changing, for to confirm all things a man plucked off his shoe and gave it to his neighbour. And this was a testimony in Israel. Therefore the kinsman said unto Boaz, "Buy it for thee." So he drew off his shoe.

And Boaz said unto the elders and unto all the people, "Ye are witnesses this day that I have bought all that was Elimelech's, and all that was Chilion's and Mahlon's, of the hand of Naomi. Moreover Ruth the Moabitess, the wife of Mahlon, have I purchased to be my wife, to raise up the name of the dead upon his inheritance that the name of the dead be not cut off from among his brethren and from the gate of his place. Ye are witnesses this day."

And all the people that were in the gate, and the elders, said, "We are witnesses."

Now the word of the Lord came unto Jonah, the son of Amittai, saying, "Arise, go to Nineveh, that great city, and cry against it, for their wickedness is come up before me."

But Jonah rose up to flee unto Tarshish from the presence of the Lord, and went down to Joppa. And he found a ship going to Tarshish, so he paid the fare thereof and went down into it, to go with them unto Tarshish from the presence of the Lord.

But the Lord sent out a great wind into the sea, and there was a mighty tempest in the sea, so that the ship was like to be broken. Then the mariners were afraid, and cried every man unto his god, and cast forth the wares that were in the ship into the sea, to lighten it of them. But Jonah was gone down into the sides of the ship, and he lay fast asleep.

So the shipmaster came to him and said unto him, "What meanest thou, O sleeper? Arise, call upon thy God, if so be that God will think upon us, that we perish not."

And they said every one to his fellow, "Come, and let us cast lots that we may know for whose cause this evil is upon us."

So they cast lots, and the lot fell upon Jonah.

Then they said unto him, "Tell us, we pray thee, for whose cause this evil is upon us? What is thine occupation? And whence comest thou? What is thy country? And of what people art thou?"

And he said unto them, "I am an Hebrew; and I fear the Lord, the God of heaven, which hath made the sea and the dry land."

Then were the men exceedingly afraid and said unto him, "Why hast thou done this?" For the men knew that he fled from the presence of the Lord because he had told them. Then they said unto him, "What shall we do unto thee, that the sea may be calm unto us?" For the sea wrought and was tempestuous.

And Jonah said unto them, "Take me up and cast me forth into the sea; so shall the sea be calm unto you, for I know that for my sake this great tempest is upon you."

Nevertheless the men rowed hard to bring it to the land, but they could not. For the sea wrought and was tempestuous against them.

Wherefore they cried unto the Lord and said, "We beseech thee, O Lord, we beseech thee, let us not perish for this man's life, and lay not upon us innocent blood, for thou, O Lord, hast done as it pleased thee."

So they took up Jonah and cast him forth into the sea, and the sea ceased from her raging. Then the men feared the Lord exceedingly, and offered a sacrifice unto the Lord, and made vows.

Now the Lord had prepared a great fish to swallow up Jonah. And Jonah was in the belly of the fish three days and three nights. And the Lord spake unto the fish, and it vomited out Jonah upon the dry land.

And the word of the Lord came unto Jonah the second time, saying, "Arise, go unto Nineveh, that great city, and preach unto it the preaching that I bid thee."

So Jonah arose and went unto Nineveh, according to the word of the Lord. Now Nineveh was an exceeding great city of three days' journey. And Jonah began to enter into the city a day's journey, and he cried and said, "Yet forty days, and Nineveh shall be overthrown."

So the people of Nineveh believed God, and proclaimed a fast and put on sackcloth, from the greatest of them even to the least of them. For word came unto the king of Nineveh, and he arose from his throne, and he laid his robe from him and covered him with sackcloth, and sat in ashes.

And he caused it to be proclaimed and published through Nineveh by the decree of the king and his nobles, saying, "Let neither man nor beast, herd nor flock, taste any thing; let them not feed nor drink water; but let man and beast be covered with sackcloth and cry mightily unto God; yea, let them turn every one from his evil way and from the violence that is in their hands. Who can tell if God will turn and repent, and turn away from his fierce anger, that we perish not?"

And God saw their works, that they turned from their

evil way; and God repented of the evil that he had said that he would do unto them, and he did it not.

But it displeased Jonah exceedingly, and he was very angry. And he prayed unto the Lord and said, "I pray thee, O Lord, was not this my saying when I was yet in my country? Therefore I fled before unto Tarshish, for I knew that thou art a gracious God, and merciful, slow to anger, and of great kindness, and repentest thee of the evil. Therefore now, O Lord, take, I beseech thee, my life from me, for it is better for me to die than to live."

Then said the Lord, "Doest thou well to be angry?"

So Jonah went out of the city and sat on the east side of the city, and there made him a booth and sat under it in the shadow, till he might see what would become of the city. And the Lord God prepared a gourd and made it to come up over Jonah, that it might be a shadow over his head, to deliver him from his grief. So Jonah was exceeding glad of the gourd.

But God prepared a worm when the morning rose the next day, and it smote the gourd, that it withered. And it came to pass, when the sun did arise, that God prepared a vehement east wind; and the sun beat upon the head of Jonah, that he fainted, and wished in himself to die, and said:

"It is better for me to die than to live."

And God said to Jonah, "Doest thou well to be angry for the gourd?"

And he said, "I do well to be angry, even unto death."

Then said the Lord, "Thou hast had pity on the gourd, for the which thou hast not laboured, neither madest it grow, which came up in a night and perished in a night. And should not I spare Nineveh, that great city, wherein are more than sixscore thousand persons that cannot discern between their right hand and their left hand; and also much cattle?"

My beloved spake and said unto me, "Rise up, my love, my fair one, and come away. For, lo, the winter is past, the rain is over and gone. The flowers appear on the earth; the time of the singing of birds is come, and the voice of the turtle is heard in our land.

"The fig tree putteth forth her green figs, and the vines with the tender grape give a good smell. Arise, my love, my fair one, and come away. O my dove, that art in the clefts of the rock, in the secret places of the stairs, let me see thy countenance, let me hear thy voice, for sweet is thy voice, and thy countenance is comely. Take us the foxes, the little foxes, that spoil the vines, for our vines have tender grapes."

My beloved is mine and I am his; he feedeth among the lilies.

My Beloved
SONG OF
SOLOMON

Make a joyful noise unto the Lord, all ye lands!
    Serve the Lord with gladness!
  Come before his presence with singing!

Know ye that the Lord he is God.
   It is he that hath made us, and not we ourselves;
   We are his people, and the sheep of his pasture.

Enter into his gates with thanksgiving,
   And into his courts with praise.
   Be thankful unto him, and bless his name.

For the Lord is good;
   His mercy is everlasting;
   And his truth endureth to all generations.

Psalm 100

PSALMS

To every thing there is a season, and a time to every purpose under the heaven:

A time to be born, and a time to die; a time to plant, and a time to pluck up that which is planted;

A time to kill, and a time to heal; a time to break down, and a time to build up;

A time to weep, and a time to laugh; a time to mourn, and a time to dance;

A time to cast away stones, and a time to gather stones together; a time to embrace, and a time to refrain from embracing;

A time to get, and a time to lose; a time to keep, and a time to cast away;

A time to rend, and a time to sew; a time to keep silence, and a time to speak;

A time to love, and a time to hate; a time of war, and a time of peace.

What profit hath he that worketh in that wherein he laboureth?

I have seen the travail which God hath given to the sons of men to be exercised in it. He hath made every thing beautiful in his time; also he hath set the world in their heart, so that no man can find out the work that God maketh from the beginning to the end.

"A TIME OF WAR"—DAVID'S SON ABSALOM

Blessed is the man
That walketh not in the counsel of the ungodly,
Nor standeth in the way of sinners,
Nor sitteth in the seat of the scornful.
But his delight is in the law of the Lord;
And in his law doth he meditate day and night.

And he shall be like a tree,
Planted by the rivers of water,
That bringeth forth his fruit in his season;
His leaf also shall not wither;
And whatsoever he doeth shall prosper.

Psalm I

PSALMS

The ungodly are not so,
But are like the chaff which the wind driveth away.
Therefore the ungodly shall not stand in the judgment,
Nor sinners in the congregation of the righteous.
For the Lord knoweth the way of the righteous,
But the way of the ungodly shall perish.

Who can find a virtuous woman? For her price is far above rubies.

The heart of her husband doth safely trust in her, so that he shall have no need of spoil.

She will do him good and not evil all the days of her life.

She seeketh wool and flax, and worketh willingly with her hands.

She is like the merchants' ships: she bringeth her food from afar.

She riseth also while it is yet night and giveth meat to her household, and a portion to her maidens.

She considereth a field and buyeth it; with the fruit of her hands she planteth a vineyard.

She girdeth her loins with strength and strengtheneth her arms.

She perceiveth that her merchandise is good: her candle goeth not out by night.

She layeth her hands to the spindle, and her hands hold the distaff.

She stretcheth out her hand to the poor; yea, she reacheth forth her hands to the needy.

She is not afraid of the snow for her household, for all her household are clothed with scarlet.

She maketh herself coverings of tapestry; her clothing is silk and purple.

Her husband is known in the gates, when he sitteth among the elders of the land.

She maketh fine linen and selleth it, and delivereth girdles unto the merchant.

"SHE BRINGETH HER FOOD FROM AFAR"

Strength and honour are her clothing, and she shall rejoice in time to come.

She openeth her mouth with wisdom, and in her tongue is the law of kindness.

She looketh well to the ways of her household and eateth not the bread of idleness.

Her children arise up and call her blessed; her husband also, and he praiseth her.

Many daughters have done virtuously, but thou excellest them all.

Favour is deceitful and beauty is vain, but a woman that feareth the Lord, she shall be praised.

Give her of the fruit of her hands and let her own works praise her in the gates.

A Virtuous Woman
PROVERBS
241

Trust in the Lord with all thine heart; and lean not unto thine own understanding.

In all thy ways acknowledge him, and he shall direct thy paths.

The spirit of man is the candle of the Lord, searching all the inward parts of the belly.

The fining pot is for silver and the furnace for gold, but the Lord trieth the hearts.

These six things doth the Lord hate: yea, seven are an abomination unto him: A proud look, a lying tongue, and hands that shed innocent blood, an heart that deviseth wicked imaginations, feet that be swift in running to mischief, a false witness that speaketh lies, and he that soweth discord among brethren.

A man that beareth false witness against his neighbour is a maul, and a sword, and a sharp arrow.

Happy is the man that findeth wisdom and the man that getteth understanding, for the merchandise of it is better than the merchandise of silver, and the gain thereof than fine gold.

She is more precious than rubies, and all the things thou canst desire are not to be compared unto her. Length of days is in her right hand; and in her left hand riches and honour. Her ways are ways of pleasantness, and all her paths are peace. She is a tree of life to them that lay hold upon her, and happy is every one that retaineth her.

Take fast hold of instruction, let her not go. Keep her, for she is thy life.

Even a fool, when he holdeth his peace, is counted wise; and he that shutteth his lips is esteemed a man of understanding.

Go to the ant, thou sluggard; consider her ways and be wise: which, having no guide, overseer, or ruler, provideth her meat in the summer and gathereth her food in the harvest.

How long wilt thou sleep, O sluggard? When wilt thou arise out of thy sleep? Yet a little sleep, a little slumber, a little folding of the hands to sleep: so shall thy poverty come as one that travelleth, and thy want as an armed man.

The slothful man saith, "There is a lion in the way; a lion is in the streets."

As the door turneth upon his hinges, so doth the slothful upon his bed.

The slothful hideth his hand in his bosom; it grieveth him to bring it again to his mouth.

The sluggard is wiser in his own conceit than seven men that can render a reason.

He that spareth his rod hateth his son, but he that loveth him chasteneth him betimes.

Train up a child in the way he should go, and when he is old he will not depart from it.

He that refuseth instruction despiseth his own soul, but he that heareth reproof getteth understanding.

Children's children are the crown of old men; and the glory of children are their fathers.

Withdraw thy foot from thy neighbour's house, lest he be weary of thee, and so hate thee.

A good name is rather to be chosen than great riches, and loving favour rather than silver and gold.

Whoso stoppeth his ears at the cry of the poor, he also shall cry himself but shall not be heard.

A merry heart doeth good like a medicine, but a broken spirit drieth the bones.

Hope deferred maketh the heart sick, but when the desire cometh it is a tree of life.

As cold waters to a thirsty soul, so is good news from a far country.

The spirit of a man will sustain his infirmity, but a wounded spirit who can bear?

Confidence in an unfaithful man in time of trouble is like a broken tooth and a foot out of joint.

Faithful are the wounds of a friend, but the kisses of an enemy are deceitful.

A soft answer turneth away wrath, but grievous words stir up anger.

A wrathful man stirreth up strife, but he that is slow to anger appeaseth strife.

A wholesome tongue is a tree of life, but perverseness therein is a breach in the spirit.

If thine enemy be hungry, give him bread to eat; and if he be thirsty, give him water to drink, for thou shalt heap coals of fire upon his head, and the Lord shall reward thee.

A word fitly spoken is like apples of gold in pictures of silver.

Answer not a fool according to his folly, lest thou also be like unto him.

Better is little with the fear of the Lord than great treasure and trouble therewith. Better is a dinner of herbs where love is than a stalled ox and hatred therewith. Better is a dry morsel, and quietness therewith, than an house full of sacrifices with strife.

It is better to dwell in a corner of the housetop than with a brawling woman in a wide house.

As a jewel of gold in a swine's snout, so is a fair woman which is without discretion.

Pride goeth before destruction, and an haughty spirit before a fall.

He that dwelleth in the secret place of the most High,
  Shall abide under the shadow of the Almighty.
I will say of the Lord, He is my refuge and my fortress:
  My God; in him will I trust.

Surely he shall deliver thee from the snare of the fowler,
  And from the noisome pestilence.
He shall cover thee with his feathers,
  And under his wings shalt thou trust:
  His truth shall be thy shield and buckler.

Thou shalt not be afraid for the terror by night,
  Nor for the arrow that flieth by day,
Nor for the pestilence that walketh in darkness,
  Nor for the destruction that wasteth at noonday.

A thousand shall fall at thy side
  And ten thousand at thy right hand,
  But it shall not come nigh thee.
Only with thine eyes shalt thou behold
  And see the reward of the wicked.

Because thou hast made the Lord, which is my refuge,
  Even the most High, thy habitation;
There shall no evil befall thee,
  Neither shall any plague come nigh thy dwelling.

For he shall give his angels charge over thee,
  To keep thee in all thy ways.
They shall bear thee up in their hands,

Lest thou dash thy foot against a stone.

Thou shalt tread upon the lion and adder:

    The young lion and the dragon shalt thou trample under
      feet.

Because he hath set his love upon me, therefore will I deliver
    him:

    I will set him on high, because he hath known my name.

He shall call upon me and I will answer him:

    I will be with him in trouble.

    I will deliver him and honour him.

With long life will I satisfy him

    And shew him my salvation.

Psalm 91

PSALMS

THE GREEK RULE
AND THE MACCABEES

Nebuchadnezzar, the king, made an image of gold whose height was threescore cubits, and the breadth thereof six cubits. He set it up in the plain of Dura, in the province of Babylon. Then Nebuchadnezzar, the king, sent to gather together the princes, the governors, and the captains, the judges, the treasurers, the counsellors, the sheriffs, and all the rulers of the provinces, to come to the dedication of the image which Nebuchadnezzar, the king, had set up.

The Fiery Furnace DANIEL 248

Then an herald cried aloud, "To you it is commanded, O people, nations, and languages, that at what time ye hear the sound of the cornet, flute, harp, sackbut, psaltery, dulcimer, and all kinds of music, ye fall down and worship the golden image that Nebuchadnezzar, the king, hath set up. And whoso falleth not down and worshippeth shall the same hour be cast into the midst of a burning fiery furnace."

Therefore at that time, when all the people heard the sound of the cornet, flute, harp, sackbut, psaltery, and all kinds of music, all the people, the nations, and the languages,

fell down and worshipped the golden image that Nebuchadnezzar, the king, had set up. Wherefore at that time certain
Chaldeans came near and accused the Jews.

They spake and said to the king Nebuchadnezzar, "O
King, live for ever. There are certain Jews whom thou hast
set over the affairs of the province of Babylon: Shadrach,
Meshach, and Abednego. These men, O King, have not regarded thee, they serve not thy gods nor worship the golden
image which thou hast set up."

Then Nebuchadnezzar in his rage and fury commanded
to bring Shadrach, Meshach, and Abednego. Then they
brought these men before the king.

Nebuchadnezzar spake and said unto them, "Is it true,
O Shadrach, Meshach, and Abednego, do not ye serve my
gods nor worship the golden image which I have set up?"

Shadrach, Meshach, and Abednego answered and said,
"Our God whom we serve is able to deliver us from the
burning fiery furnace, and he will deliver us out of thine
hand, O King. But if not, be it known unto thee, O King,
that we will not serve thy gods nor worship the golden image
which thou hast set up."

Then was Nebuchadnezzar full of fury, and the form of
his visage was changed against Shadrach, Meshach, and
Abednego. Therefore he spake and commanded that they
should heat the furnace one seven times more than it was
wont to be heated. And he commanded the most mighty men
that were in his army to bind Shadrach, Meshach, and
Abednego and to cast them into the burning fiery furnace.

Then these men were bound in their coats, their hosen,
and their hats, and their other garments, and were cast into
the midst of the burning fiery furnace.

Then Nebuchadnezzar, the king, was astonied, and
rose up in haste, and spake and said unto his counsellors,

"Did not we cast three men bound into the midst of the fire?"

They answered and said unto the king, "True, O King."

He answered and said, "Lo, I see four men loose, walking in the midst of the fire, and they have no hurt; and the form of the fourth is like the Son of God."

Then Nebuchadnezzar came near to the mouth of the burning fiery furnace and spake and said, "Shadrach, Meshach, and Abednego, ye servants of the most high God, come forth, and come hither."

Then Shadrach, Meshach, and Abednego came forth of the midst of the fire. And the princes, governors, and captains, and the king's counsellors, being gathered together, saw these men, upon whose bodies the fire had no power, nor was an hair of their head singed, neither were their coats changed, nor the smell of fire had passed on them.

Then Nebuchadnezzar spake and said, "Blessed be the God of Shadrach, Meshach, and Abednego, who hath sent his angel and delivered his servants that trusted in him, and have changed the king's word, and yielded their bodies that they might not serve nor worship any god except their own God.

"Therefore I make a decree that every people, nation, and language which speak any thing amiss against the God of Shadrach, Meshach, and Abednego shall be cut in pieces and their houses shall be made a dunghill, because there is no other God that can deliver after this sort."

Then the king promoted Shadrach, Meshach, and Abednego in the province of Babylon.

Belshazzar, the king, made a great feast to a thousand of his lords, and drank wine before the thousand. Belshazzar, whiles he tasted the wine, commanded to bring the golden and silver vessels which his father, Nebuchadnezzar, had taken out of the temple which was in Jerusalem, that the king and his princes, his wives and his concubines might drink therein.

Then they brought the golden vessels that were taken out of the temple of the house of God which was at Jerusalem, and the king and his princes, his wives and his concubines drank in them. They drank wine and praised the gods of gold and of silver, of brass, of iron, of wood and of stone.

In the same hour came forth fingers of a man's hand and wrote over against the candlestick upon the plaster of the wall of the king's palace, and the king saw the part of the hand that wrote. Then the king's countenance was changed and his thoughts troubled him, so that the joints of his loins were loosed and his knees smote one against another. The king cried aloud to bring in the astrologers, the Chaldeans, and the soothsayers.

And the king spake and said to the wise men of Babylon, "Whosoever shall read this writing and shew me the interpretation thereof shall be clothed with scarlet and have a chain of gold about his neck and shall be the third ruler in the kingdom."

Then came in all the king's wise men, but they could not read the writing nor make known to the king the interpretation thereof. Then was the king Belshazzar greatly troubled, and his countenance was changed in him, and his lords were astonied.

Now the queen, by reason of the words of the king and his lords, came into the banquet house. And the queen spake and said, "O King, live for ever. Let not thy thoughts trouble thee nor let thy countenance be changed. There is a man in thy kingdom in whom is understanding and wisdom like the wisdom of the gods. Now let Daniel be called, and he will shew the interpretation."

Writing on
The Wall
DANIEL

Then was Daniel brought in before the king.

Then Daniel said, "Thou, O Belshazzar, hast not humbled thine heart but hast lifted up thyself against the Lord of heaven. And they have brought the vessels of his house before thee, and thou and thy lords, thy wives and thy concubines have drunk wine in them. And thou hast praised the gods of silver and gold, of brass, iron, wood, and stone, which see not, nor hear, nor know. And the God in whose hand thy breath is, and whose are all thy ways, hast thou not glorified.

"Then was part of the hand sent from him, and this writing was written. And this is the writing that was written: MENE, MENE, TEKEL, UPHARSIN. This is the interpretation of the thing: MENE, God hath numbered thy kingdom and finished it. TEKEL, Thou art weighed in the balances and art found wanting. PERES, Thy kingdom is divided and given to the Medes and Persians."

In that night was Belshazzar, the king of the Chaldeans, slain. And Darius the Median took the kingdom, being about threescore and two years old.

It pleased Darius to set over the kingdom an hundred and twenty princes which should be over the whole kingdom; and over these three presidents, of whom Daniel was first. Then this Daniel was preferred above the presidents and princes because an excellent spirit was in him, and the king thought to set him over the whole realm.

Then the presidents and princes sought to find occasion against Daniel concerning the kingdom, but they could find none occasion nor fault, forasmuch as he was faithful, neither was there any error or fault found in him.

Then said these men, "We shall not find any occasion against this Daniel except we find it against him concerning the law of his God."

Then these presidents and princes assembled together to the king and said thus unto him: "King Darius, live for ever. All the presidents of the kingdom, the governors and the princes, the counsellors and the captains have consulted together to establish a royal statute and to make a firm decree that whosoever shall ask a petition of any God or man for thirty days, save of thee, O King, he shall be cast into the den of lions. Now, O King, establish the decree and sign the writing, that it be not changed, according to the law of the Medes and Persians, which altereth not." Wherefore King Darius signed the writing and the decree.

Now when Daniel knew that the writing was signed he went into his house; and, his windows being open in his chamber toward Jerusalem, he kneeled upon his knees three times a day, and prayed and gave thanks before his God, as he did aforetime.

Then these men assembled and found Daniel praying and making supplication before his God.

Then they came near and spake before the king: "Daniel, which is of the children of the captivity of Judah, regardeth not thee, O King, nor the decree that thou hast signed, but maketh his petition three times a day."

Then the king, when he heard these words, was sore displeased with himself and set his heart on Daniel to deliver him, and he laboured till the going down of the sun to deliver him.

Then these men assembled unto the king and said unto the king, "Know, O King, that the law of the Medes and

Persians is, 'That no decree nor statute which the king establisheth may be changed.'"

Then the king commanded, and they brought Daniel and cast him into the den of lions.

Now the king spake and said unto Daniel, "Thy God, whom thou servest continually, he will deliver thee."

And a stone was brought and laid upon the mouth of the den, and the king sealed it with his own signet and with the signet of his lords, that the purpose might not be changed concerning Daniel. Then the king went to his palace and passed the night fasting; neither were instruments of music brought before him; and his sleep went from him.

Then the king arose very early in the morning and went in haste unto the den of lions. And when he came to the den he cried with a lamentable voice unto Daniel.

And the king spake and said to Daniel, "O Daniel, servant of the living God, is thy God, whom thou servest continually, able to deliver thee from the lions?"

Then said Daniel unto the king, "O King, live for ever. My God hath sent his angel and hath shut the lions' mouths that they have not hurt me."

In the first year of Belshazzar, king of Babylon, Daniel had a dream and visions of his head upon his bed. Then he wrote the dream and told the sum of the matters.

"I saw in the night visions, and, behold, one like the Son of Man came with the clouds of heaven and came to the Ancient of Days, and they brought him near before him. And there was given him dominion and glory and a kingdom, that all people, nations, and languages should serve him. His dominion is an everlasting dominion which shall not pass away, and his kingdom that which shall not be destroyed."

He will swallow up death in victory, and the Lord God will wipe away tears from off all faces, and the rebuke of his people shall he take away from off all the earth, for the Lord hath spoken it.

And it shall be said in that day, "Lo, this is our God; we have waited for him, and he will save us. This is the Lord; we have waited for him, we will be glad and rejoice in his salvation."

Life Eternal

ISAIAH

256

The Picture that Mom Drew

written and illustrated by
Kathy Mallat

written and photo-illustrated by
Bruce McMillan

WALKER AND COMPANY NEW YORK

"This is our mom.

This is the paper
used for the picture
that Mom drew.

These are the **colors**

that brightened the paper

used for the picture

that Mom drew.

These are some l i n e s

sketched with the **colors**

that brightened the paper

used for the picture

that Mom drew.

These are some shapes

drawn with the l i n e s

sketched with the colors

that brightened the paper

used for the picture

that Mom drew.

These are some **forms**

molded from the shapes

drawn with the l i n e s

sketched with the **colors**

that brightened the paper

used for the picture

that Mom drew.

These are some **shades**

layered over the **forms**

molded from the shapes

drawn with the l i n e s

sketched with the **colors**

that brightened the paper

used for the picture

that Mom drew.

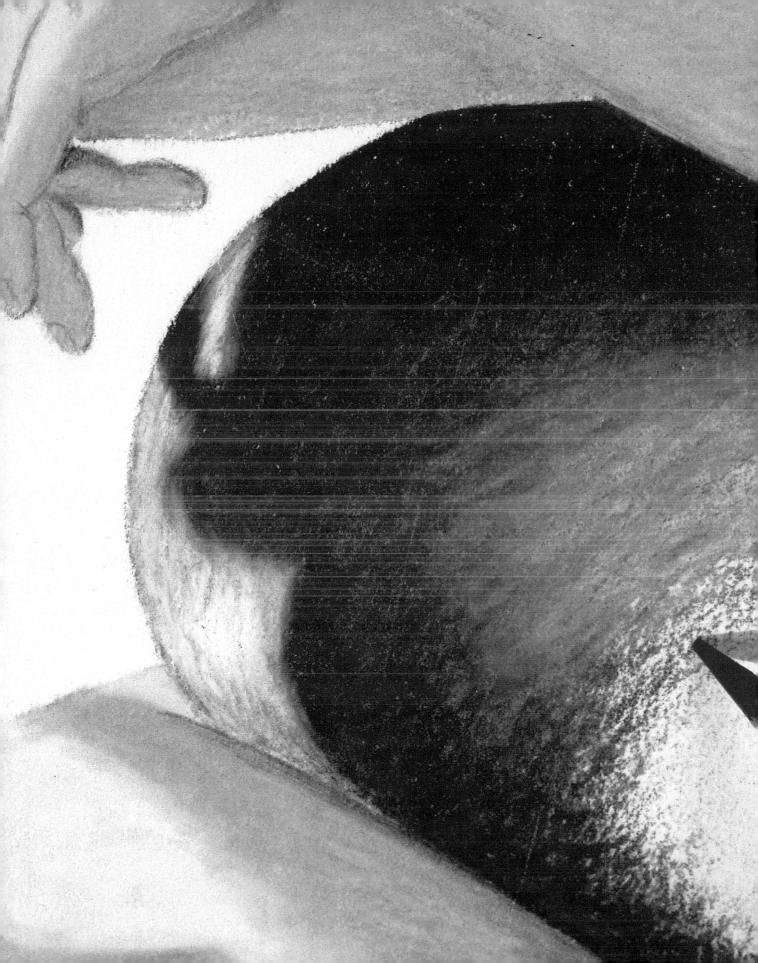

These are some **patterns**

enhanced by the **shades**

layered over the **forms**

molded from the shapes

drawn with the l i n e s

sketched with the **colors**

that brightened the paper

used for the picture

that Mom drew.

These are some textures

next to the patterns

enhanced by the shades

layered over the forms

molded from the shapes

drawn with the l i n e s

sketched with the colors

that brightened the paper

used for the picture

that Mom drew, and...

this is the picture

that Mom drew."

The Elements of Art that Mom Used

Colors are reflected light waves. Substances that reflect colors–pigments–are used to make colored pencils, paints, and even the inks used to print this book.

The **primary colors** are red, blue, and yellow.

The **secondary colors** are purple, green, and orange. They are made by mixing two primary colors together. Red and blue make purple. Blue and yellow make green. Red and yellow make orange.

Warm colors, such as reds, yellows, or oranges, sometimes evoke a feeling of warmth.

Cool colors, such as blues, greens, or violets, sometimes evoke a feeling of cold.

Lines are long narrow marks.

Shapes are areas with an outline, such as circles, squares, rectangles, and triangles, that have only two dimensions, height and width.

Forms are three dimensional spaces with an outline, such as spheres, cylinders, cubes, and pyramids, that have height, width, and depth.

Shades are gradual changes of a color from dark to light.

Patterns are a rhythmic repetition of lines, shapes, forms, or colors.

Textures show the way surfaces feel, such as smooth, rough, or bumpy.

For my dad, David W. Sherburne —K.M.
For my high school art teacher, Marylyn Wentworth —B.M.

A Note from the Authors

The two girls in the picture, Erin and her younger sister, Meghan, are the daughters of Kathy and Steve Mallat. They were photographed at a secluded coastal beach in southern Maine. Kathy's drawings were made using Berol Prismacolor colored pencils on Strathmore 500 Series Bristol Board paper. Bruce's photographs were made using a Nikon F4 camera with an MF23 back set to bracket exposures, and a 105 mm f 2.8 micro Nikon lens, either with no filter, a light blue filter, or polarizing filter. An aluminum foil reflector for fill light was used in all photos. The book was designed by Bruce, using Optima for text type, and both Arab Brush and a redrawn Gill Sans for display type.

Kathy Mallat   *Bruce McMillan*

First published in the United States of America in 1997
by Walker Publishing Company, Inc.

Published simultaneously in Canada by
Thomas Allen & Son Canada,
Limited, Markham, Ontario

Library of Congress Cataloging-in-Publication Data
Mallat, Kathy.
The picture that Mom drew/written and illustrated by Kathy Mallat;
written and photo-illustrated by Bruce McMillan.   p. cm.
Summary: Introduces the seven basic elements of art by using
colored pencils to add colors, lines, shapes, forms, shades,
patterns, and textures one at a time to a piece of paper.
ISBN 0-8027-8617-0 (hardcover: alk. paper).
—ISBN 0-8027-8618-9 (reinforced: alk. paper)
1. Colored pencil drawing—Technique—Juvenile literature.
[1. Colored pencil drawing—Technique. 2. Drawing—Technique.]
I. McMillan, Bruce. II. Title.
NC892.M35 1997 741.2′4—DC20 96-30165 CIP AC

Printed in Hong Kong

2 4 6 8 10 9 7 5 3 1